# Drone War Vietnam

# Drone War Vietnam

David Axe

Pen & Sword
**MILITARY**

First published in Great Britain in 2021 by
Pen & Sword Military
An imprint of
Pen & Sword Books Ltd
Yorkshire – Philadelphia

Copyright © David Axe 2021

ISBN 978 1 52677 026 4

The right of David Axe to be identified as Author of this work has been asserted by him in accordance with the Copyright, Designs and Patents Act 1988.

A CIP catalogue record for this book is available from the British Library.

All rights reserved. No part of this book may be reproduced or transmitted in any form or by any means, electronic or mechanical including photocopying, recording or by any information storage and retrieval system, without permission from the Publisher in writing.

Typeset by Mac Style
Printed and bound in India by
Replika Press Pvt. Ltd.

Pen & Sword Books Limited incorporates the imprints of Atlas, Archaeology, Aviation, Discovery, Family History, Fiction, History, Maritime, Military, Military Classics, Politics, Select, Transport,
True Crime, Air World, Frontline Publishing, Leo Cooper, Remember When, Seaforth Publishing, The Praetorian Press, Wharncliffe
Local History, Wharncliffe Transport, Wharncliffe True Crime and White Owl.

For a complete list of Pen & Sword titles please contact

**PEN & SWORD BOOKS LIMITED**
47 Church Street, Barnsley, South Yorkshire, S70 2AS, England
E-mail: enquiries@pen-and-sword.co.uk
Website: www.pen-and-sword.co.uk

Or

**PEN AND SWORD BOOKS**
1950 Lawrence Rd, Havertown, PA 19083, USA
E-mail: Uspen-and-sword@casematepublishers.com
Website: www.penandswordbooks.com

# Contents

*About the Author* — vi
*Introduction* — vii

**Chapter One** — 1

**Chapter Two** — 9

**Chapter Three** — 27

**Chapter Four** — 38

**Chapter Five** — 43

**Chapter Six** — 50

**Chapter Seven** — 63

**Chapter Eight** — 69

**Chapter Nine** — 79

**Chapter Ten** — 86

**Chapter Eleven** — 95

**Chapter Twelve** — 106

**Chapter Thirteen** — 121

**Chapter Fourteen** — 127

**Chapter Fifteen** — 135

**Chapter Sixteen** — 144

*Bibliography/Sources* — 160
*Index* — 162

# About the Author

David Axe is a journalist and filmmaker in Columbia, South Carolina. A contributor to The Daily Beast, Vice, Reuters, Wired.com, *The Village Voice*, *The Washington Post* and many other publications, David also has blogged for Forbes as well as for several websites he created. David has written and edited several non-fiction books, most recently the 2017 graphic novel war memoir *Machete Squad*. He has written or directed several movies, including *The Theta Girl* (2017), *Shed* (2019) and *Lection* (2020).

# Introduction

On October 7, 2001, a US Air Force MQ-1 Predator drone flying over Afghanistan fired a missile at a building CIA analysts suspected of housing Taliban leader Mullah Omar. The Predator missed and instead struck a vehicle, killing several of the mullah's bodyguards.

The botched Predator strike was hardly the first time US military and intelligence agencies had sent aerial robots into battle. As early as the Second World War, the military had tinkered with remote-controlled bombers.

Drones also played an important – and today largely unheralded – role in the bloody, two-decade US air war over Vietnam and surrounding countries in the 1960s and '70s. Drone aircraft spotted targets for manned US bombers, jammed North Vietnamese radars and scattered propaganda leaflets, among other missions.

This book explores that obscure chapter of history. *DRONE WAR VIETNAM* is based on military records, official histories and published first-hand accounts from early drone operators, as well as on a close survey of existing scholarship on the topic.

The Ryan Aeronautical Model 147 Lightning Bug subsonic drone, a mainstay of the Vietnam air war, launched in mid-air from a DC-130 motherplane and, at the end of its mission, popped a parachute and floated toward the ground. A helicopter buzzed in to retrieve it.

The Model 147s were crude, unreliable and vulnerable to enemy air defenses and espionage. In 1967 the North Vietnamese began intercepting the drone operators' radio signals and exploited the resulting intelligence to set aerial ambushes for drones and manned warplanes. Spiking losses forced the Air Force and the National Security Agency to equip the motherships with new radio encryption.

The Lightning Bug evolved. By the end of the war new Model 147s were more effective, more reliable and more survivable than early models, and they inspired totally new drone designs that further improved on the basic concept of unmanned aerial reconnaissance.

In perhaps the ultimate expression of robotic recce up to that point, the CIA deployed supersonic drones to spy on Vietnam's neighbors. After many failures, the powerful D-21 drone – in essence a pilotless miniature of the Mach-3 SR-71 manned spy plane – photographed China's Lop Nor nuclear test site between 1969 and 1971.

After Saigon fell to North Vietnamese forces in 1975, the Pentagon quickly cooled on drones. The advent of more capable and more reliable satellites arguably rendered obsolete the drones that flew over Vietnam and its neighbors. For four decades, fast and dumb spy drones with their volatile engines, self-contained navigation systems and general lack of real-time data-link to their operators were … historical curiosities.

Then history began to loop back on itself. The high cost and inherent limitations of spy satellites in the 1990s spurred the development of a new generation of combat drone. The Predator that fired on Mullah Omar in October 2001 dramatically announced what appeared to many to be a whole new kind of warfare.

Yet it wasn't new. In their fledgling efforts to send robots instead of human beings on the most dangerous aerial missions, US operators in South-East Asia in the 1960s and '70s wrote the first chapter in the continuing tale of autonomous warfare.

# Chapter One

The story of American drones over Vietnam doesn't begin in Vietnam.

Not in August 1964 when North Vietnamese torpedo boats allegedly attacked the US Navy destroyer USS *Maddox* in the Gulf of Tonkin, spurring President Lyndon Johnson to order retaliatory air strikes and the US Congress to authorize a wider war effort.

Nor even in May 1961 when President John F. Kennedy deployed US Army helicopters and Green Berets to South Vietnam for secret operations targeting Viet Cong guerrillas.

No, it begins much earlier in a much colder country, in the Soviet Union in 1950.

That year, Soviet military leaders realized they had a problem. The US Air Force at the time possessed around 1,000 bombers with the range and payload to drop the United States' roughly 300 atomic bombs on cities across the Soviet Union.

The Soviet Air Force, by contrast, possessed a few hundred obsolete bombers as well as around five atomic bombs. The bomber gap favored the Americans by a huge margin and prevented deterrence by way of mutually-assured destruction (MAD).

The American threat wasn't only nuclear. The devastation that US Air Force B-29s rained on North Korea starting in mid-1950 particularly alarmed Soviet premier Joseph Stalin.

The Soviets needed to fortify their cities against the apocalyptic threat of American atomic bombers. As many Cold War weapons-developers did when faced with a profound technological problem, they looked to Nazi Germany for solutions.

Near the end of the Second World War in 1945, German scientists, desperate to defend against hordes of Allied bombers, were on the cusp of developing radar-guided surface-to-air missiles (SAMs). The Soviet Union scooped up some of that early SAM technology – and more than a few Nazi scientists – and launched the development of a copycat system.

The copycat system ultimately never entered service, but it did inspire a rival program to develop the Berkut SAM network. In August 1950, Stalin ordered the Kremlin to deploy the Berkut system around Moscow within one year. He wanted the system to be able to stop a 1,000-bomber raid like the kind the Allies occasionally mounted late in the Second World War.

In fact, it took eight years for workers to finish building Berkut. Stalin's death in 1953 and the subsequent violent purge of many of his closest allies contributed to the delay, but the system's sheer scale was the main reason it took so long to complete. Following the purge, Berkut became known as the S-25.

The S-25 was, in the words of historian Steven Zaloga, 'an immense undertaking'. It consisted of a staggering fifty-six missile regiments in two concentric rings around Moscow. To support the missile sites, prison laborers built two ring roads around Moscow that, according to a US intelligence assessment, required as much concrete as the entire Soviet economy typically consumed in a year. The ring roads have become fixtures of Moscow's modern transport system.

Beside the launchers, each S-25 site included 60 launch pads for V-300 missiles, a B-200 radar, a command bunker and crew housing and covered around 360 acres, usually in a forested area. It took almost 500 officers and men to staff a single site.

Standing 39ft tall with a warhead weighing up to 700lb, the V-300 – or SA-1, as NATO referred to it – was a monster of a missile, but it was inaccurate. It was standard practice for crews to fire three missiles at a time on the assumption that two would widely miss their target. Anticipating huge defensive barrages during wartime, by 1958 the Kremlin bought no fewer than 32,000 V-300 missiles.

The S-25 system had another fatal flaw. It worked best when engaging targets flying below 59,000ft. However, the new U-2 spy plane that the US Central Intelligence Agency (CIA) and US Air Force began operating in 1956 could fly higher than 70,000ft.

Soviet air defense planners had little faith in the S-25, and not only because the V-300 missile lacked performance. 'The system layout was ill-conceived, being spaced equally around the periphery of Moscow,' Zaloga explained. 'This meant that at the most likely points of bomber attack, the north and west, the thin layer of defenses could be overwhelmed during an attack, or the defenses breached by preliminary attacks prior to the main bomber waves.'

The S-25 lingered in service through the early 1980s, but neither country that deployed the system – the Soviet Union and North Korea – ever fired a V-300 missile in anger. For front-line use in actual shooting wars, the Soviets developed a much better air defense system, one that would shape a generation of American reconnaissance technology.

This was the S-75, NATO code-name SA-2. Soviet planners rushed development of the S-75, starting in 1954. While it borrowed some components from the S-25 system, the S-75 was simpler and easier to transport. Its SNR-75 radar took advantage of recent technological advancements. The two-stage V-750 missile, 35ft from tip to tail, was more powerful and more accurate than the V-300. It could hit targets 28 miles away. Perhaps most importantly, it worked at altitudes higher than 70,000ft.

In July 1956, the S-25 system around Moscow detected, for the first time, one of the CIA's U-2s flying with impunity over Moscow. Soviet premier Nikita Khrushchev, duly enraged, ordered the Kremlin to speed up the S-75's development. Shoot down the U-2s, Khrushchev demanded. Meanwhile, Soviet diplomats filed a formal complaint to the US embassy in Moscow about the U-2 overflights.

US president Dwight Eisenhower was upset. Richard Bissell, Jr, the CIA official who oversaw Lockheed's work on the U-2, had assured Eisenhower that Soviet radars wouldn't detect the U-2.

When that rosy prediction proved false, Eisenhower suspended the CIA's authority to approve U-2 flights over the Soviet Union. Moving forward, the president would approve, on an individual basis, each U-2 mission over Soviet territory. Eisenhower rejected more proposed U-2 sorties than he approved.

There was just one U-2 mission over the Soviet Union in 1958 and two in 1959. In early 1960 Eisenhower promised Khrushchev that there would be no U-2 flights over the Soviet Union during the remaining months of his administration ending in January 1961.

The first V-750 missiles entered service in 1957. Soon S-75 systems were in place around Moscow, Leningrad and Baku. As thousands of V-750s poured from Soviet factories, the Kremlin's developers were hard at work improving the missile and its associated radars. In 1958 the Soviet Union exported to China five batteries of S-75s and deployed technicians to help operate the systems. A year later, everything changed.

As part of a proxy spying effort targeting the Communist Bloc, the United States had equipped the Taiwanese military with high-altitude spy planes including RB-57s and U-2s. On October 7, 1959, a salvo of three V-750s destroyed a Taiwanese RB-57 flying over China at an altitude of 65,600ft. It was the first-ever hostile shoot-down of an aircraft by a surface-to-air missile.

A little over a month later on November 16, 1959, a Soviet S-75 battery shot down an American WS-416L reconnaissance balloon, Zaloga claimed. 'This incident remains unverified,' he noted.

In mid-1960 Eisenhower made a fateful decision. Under pressure to better understand Soviet ballistic missile developments and frustrated with delays in the Corona spy-satellite program, the president approved a U-2 mission over the Soviet Union, this despite his pledge to the Soviet premier. On May 1, 1960, CIA pilot Gary Francis Powers took off from a base in Pakistan and winged toward the Ukraine, a center of Soviet weapons production.

Soviet radars tracked the U-2 the whole way. A dozen Soviet fighters climbed to intercept but couldn't reach the high-flying U-2. Powers' luck ran out near Sverdlovsk. A nearby factory produced the latest 13D version of the V-750 missile. Local S-75 batteries were among the first to receive the new, more powerful 13D.

Two S-75 batteries launched missiles at the U-2. One 13D exploded behind the spy plane at an altitude of 67,000ft. The damaged U-2 spiraled out of control. Powers bailed out right before a second V-750 struck his plane.

Powers' shoot-down sparked a diplomatic crisis, one that the Pentagon and the White House had anticipated. 'Someone had better be giving some thought to the problem we're going to have if and when a U-2 pilot comes down in unfriendly territory,' Colonel Harold Wood, the Air Force's head of reconnaissance, said at a meeting with his deputy Lieutenant Colonel Lloyd Ryan in the Pentagon basement in September 1959.

That someone turned out to be Ray Ballweg, vice president of Pasadena-based Hycon Manufacturing, which produced the U-2's powerful cameras.

A few weeks after Wood uttered his ominous warning, Ballweg met the colonel and his deputy at the Pentagon. Ryan echoed Wood's concern about the seeming inevitability of a U-2 pilot winding up in enemy hands.

'Hell, Lloyd, why don't you have us install a camera in a jet target drone?' Ballweg said. 'No reason it can't be programmed to do the recon job for you and bring back pictures.' No pilot, no risk of a pilot getting captured. However, Wood and Ryan knew nothing about unmanned aircraft. 'What drone?' Ryan recalled saying. Ballweg mentioned Ryan Aeronautical Company in San Diego.

The Lockheed U-2 spy plane began flying with the US Central Intelligence Agency and US Air Force in 1956. Richard Bissell, Jr, the CIA official who oversaw Lockheed's work on the U-2, assured President Dwight Eisenhower that Soviet radars wouldn't detect the U-2. (*US Air Force photo*)

Hycon developed the U-2's A-2 camera system in the late 1950s. Each set included three HR732 cameras. To produce an HR732, Hycon took an existing aerial reconnaissance camera with its 24in focal length and modified it to withstand the cold temperature and low air pressure that a U-2 encountered at altitudes over 60,000ft. (*US Air Force photo*)

Technicians load a set of Hycon Model 732 cameras into a U-2's equipment bay. The set weighed nearly 340lb. Hycon adapted the HR732 for use on the Model 147 drone, redesignating it the HR233. Whereas a U-2 with its capacious camera bay and big engine and wing could loft three HR732s, each weighing more than 110lb, the Model 147 drone could carry just one HR233, and the drone's camera came fitted with a smaller lens than was on the U-2's cameras. The Model 147's camera also produced a smaller negative than the U-2's. The drone finally got a second camera in 1966 when Ryan Aeronautical added a small KA-60 panoramic camera to the low-flying Model 147J. (*US Air Force photo*)

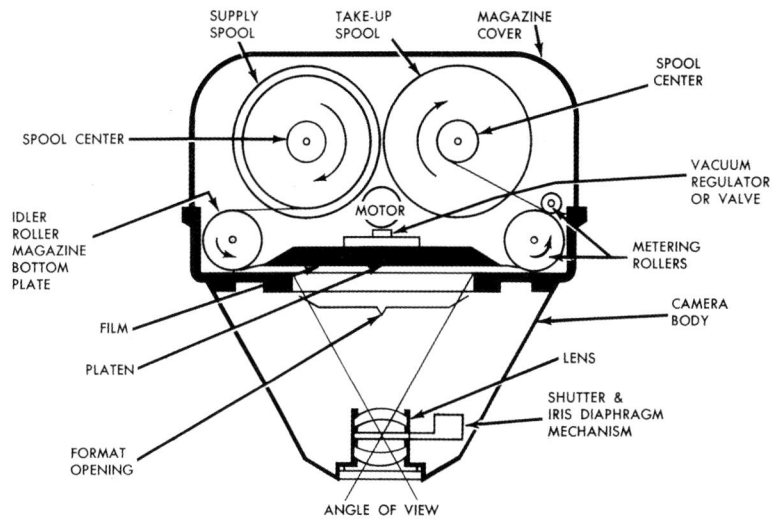

The individual HR732s in the U-2's A-2 set could distinguish objects as small as 2ft across from a height of more than 12 miles, greatly improving on earlier aerial-reconnaissance cameras that, with their shorter focal lengths, could distinguish objects 25ft across at 6 miles of altitude. Each camera in the A-2 set could carry 1,800ft of Eastman Kodak's lightweight Mylar-based film, which produced 9in by 18in negatives. (*US Air Force art*)

In July 1965 the Soviet Union formally agreed to supply S-75 surface-to-air missile systems to North Vietnam. By then a Soviet-led training program for Vietnamese missile crews was already well under way in the Soviet Union as well as at ten camps in North Vietnam. Soviet-supplied, Soviet-staffed and Soviet-led North Vietnamese S-75 batteries entered combat on July 24, 1965, when two batteries of the 236th SAM Regiment near Hanoi fired on a flight of US Air Force F-4C fighters, shooting down one jet. (*US Air Force photo*)

A North Vietnamese V-750 missile strikes a US Air Force RF–4C reconnaissance plane over Hanoi on August 12, 1967. Captains Edwin Atterberry and Thomas Parrott ejected and were captured. Atterberry died in a North Vietnamese prison. Parrott was released at the end of the war. (*US Air Force photo*)

# Chapter Two

Founded in 1934 by airline pioneer T.C. Ryan, Ryan Aeronautical built training planes during the Second World War. Post-war, the firm turned its attention to missiles and rockets.

In 1948 the company won the Air Force's first-ever contract to build pilotless aircraft. Just shy of 9ft long with a span of 12.5ft, the original Q-2 Firebee drone with its Continental J-69 engine could reach 521 knots at a maximum altitude of 40,000ft. The American and Canadian militaries bought more than 4,000 Q-2s for use as aerial targets. Launch them, shoot them down.

Yet the reliable little drone could do so much more than that, Ballweg believed. 'That bird's proven to be a pretty stable aerial platform – just what you need when flying a camera,' Ballweg said of the Firebee. It just so happened that a Ryan representative was scheduled, in a few weeks' time, to brief Pentagon officials on the Q-2. Ballweg urged Wood and Ryan to attend the briefing.

They did. The briefing, by Ryan Aeronautical's Bill Orr, detailed the capabilities of the company's new Q-2C drone, a bigger and more powerful version of the 1948-vintage Firebee. However, Orr only discussed the drone's potential as a better-performing target for air defense training.

Ryan Aeronautical had promoted the Firebee as a potential recon vehicle as far back as 1955 but, gaining no traction, the company had abandoned the idea.

Colonel Ryan placed a telephone call to Ryan Aeronautical in an effort to stimulate interest at the company in transforming the Q-2C into a recon aircraft, but the Air Force's requirement for a new reconnaissance capability was classified. In his call, the colonel could only hint at the real reasons for his sudden interest in the Q-2C. 'Somehow nothing came of that call either,' Ryan recalled.

Ballweg ran interference on Lloyd Ryan's behalf. He negotiated a deal between Hycon and Ryan Aeronautical to co-operate on a recon drone design combining the latter's airframe with the former's camera.

Meanwhile Colonel Ryan finally succeeded in getting on the phone to the right person at Ryan Aeronautical: Edward Uhl, a Ryan Aeronautical vice president who had recently worked for Martin on that company's RB-57 manned recon plane.

Uhl understood reconnaissance and grasped what the frustrated Colonel Ryan was hinting at in his phone calls. Around Christmas 1959, Colonel Ryan told Ryan

Aeronautical to get to work on a recon drone. This wasn't the same as the Air Force cutting an actual contract. There was no guarantee that the flying branch actually would buy the drone, but Ryan Aeronautical took a chance.

The firm tapped Robert Schwanhausser to head the effort. Schwanhausser was a complex and sometimes troubled character. Born in 1930 to a wealthy family in Buffalo, New York, Schwanhausser developed a childhood fascination with two things: airplanes and girls.

Inspired by his older brother, an Army Air Force pilot during the Second World War, Schwanhausser studied aeronautics at the Massachusetts Institute of Technology then joined the Air Force. Schwanhausser was tall and ruggedly handsome. He liked women and women liked him. What few people realized was that Schwanhausser actually *identified* as a woman and sometimes wore women's clothes while in the privacy of his own home.

In 1959, Schwanhausser was skeptical that the Air Force would follow through on its verbal commitment to Ryan Aeronautical's drones. 'I don't see much future in this reconnaissance drone stuff,' Schwanhausser told Uhl.

Suffering no surfeit of optimism, Schwanhausser got to work. In early 1960 he met with top Air Force intelligence officials – the so-called 'reconnaissance panel' – at the Pentagon. After walking the officials through the twelve-year history of target drones in US military service, Schwanhausser offered an idea that, in fits and starts over the next fifty years, would transform warfare.

Versions of the same drones that the Air Force routinely shot down over its training ranges could also function as front-line warplanes, Schwanhausser explained. Fitted with cameras, a modified Firebee could fly as far as 1,400 miles to photograph enemy installations. It could be launched from the ground or from under the wing of a mothership plane. Mission complete, the drone would parachute itself to the ground or sea for retrieval by helicopter or boat.

An operational Firebee could do the same job as the U-2 and without risking a pilot and a diplomatic crisis. 'The use of U-2 manned vehicles for overflights of the territory of nations unfriendly to the United States creates, we believe, risks which are unnecessary to take,' Schwanhausser said. 'We feel there is a solution to this in the logical evolution of the unmanned Firebee drone system.'

The reconnaissance panel was impressed, but it was also broke. In the late 1950s and early 1960s the Air Force devoted the bulk of its resources to developing new, nuclear-tipped ballistic missiles.

Reconnaissance budgets, thin as they were, already covered the U-2, the top-secret SR-71, the RB-57 and a recon version of the F-101 fighter. The Corona spy satellite was also under development. There wasn't much left over for drones.

Still, the service managed to find $200,000 to pay Ryan Aeronautical to study reconnaissance drones. The study contract evolved into a larger test program the Air Force called 'Red Wagon'. Ryan Aeronautical devoted four Q-2Cs to the effort.

Red Wagon launched in the summer of 1960, but only after surviving a potentially fatal bureaucratic intervention. Courtland Perkins, the Air Force's assistant secretary for research and development, believed the program was a waste of time. Courtland phoned Ryan, the deputy reconnaissance chief, and told him to cancel Ryan Aeronautical's study contract.

Ryan didn't want to do that. He called up Ryan Aeronautical in San Diego 'to find out how far along they were,' he recalled. 'It turned out the Air Force had already committed the money, anyhow.'

So Ryan chose to ignore Perkins' telephoned order. After all, Ryan explained, Perkins never actually put his order into writing, which made it more of a recommendation than an official directive. 'We just went ahead and did the test program.'

Ryan Aeronautical started cutting subcontracts to all the companies whose help it needed testing the Q-2Cs: Hycon for cameras; Litton Industries in New Jersey for guidance systems; Lockheed was involved, as was Space Technology Labs. Schwanhausser and his staff of 100 people moved into a new facility in San Diego where they could work on their secretive program without anyone asking a lot of questions.

The goal was to evolve the Q-2C, then a mere target, into an operational reconnaissance or 'recce' aircraft. Schwanhausser explained his goals in a formal technical proposal that he delivered to the Air Force a couple of months after his meeting with the reconnaissance panel.

First, Ryan Aeronautical would need to expand the Q-2C's flying range to at least 1,100 miles in order to allow the drone to complete 'deep penetrations into the Soviet bloc,' Schwanhausser explained. That meant adding 60 gallons of fuel capacity to the basic Q-2C.

For missions over distances of 2,500 miles, Ryan Aeronautical should develop a new version of the Q-2 with a bigger wing and a new version of the J69 engine producing 2,400lb of thrust, Schwanhausser advised.

Ryan Aeronautical had already developed all the ground support equipment for the Q-2 series of drones. The company had demonstrated aerial launches from the GC-130 version of the popular Hercules transport plane. Trials of the ground-launch apparatus would take place over the summer of 1960.

Hycon set about designing a camera that balanced resolution and size. The company at the time was America's leading maker of military reconnaissance equipment. Its cameras were the products of five decades of technological improvement.

J.S. Butz summarized the state of the art in a 1963 article in *Air Force & Space Digest*. Noting that the best cameras at that time could produce images depicting 100 discernible separate line segments on a 1mm span of film – a resolution roughly equivalent in sharpness to a well-shot 35mm movie – Butz attributed the advancements in aerial photography to evolution, not revolution.

'The advances in photography are not based on any fundamentally new techniques or inventions,' Butz wrote. 'They have been brought about by a concentrated effort on improving the basic elements in a camera: the lens, the film and the shutter.'

Butz cited three rules in camera construction:

'Rule one: There is no substitute for focal length. As the film is moved back from the lens, the scale factor is decreased, i.e., one inch on the photograph represents a shorter distance on the ground.

'Rule two: There is no substitute for shutter speed. All aerial cameras must be equipped with some mechanism to compensate for the motion of the camera platform relative to the ground. Accurate image motion compensation is vital or the pictures will be blurred. The use of very fast shutter speeds is the best means of keeping this motion-compensation problem manageable.

'Rule three: Make it as big as you can.'

For the U-2 with its cockpit-size camera bay, 'big' was okay. After some unhappy experiments with multiple-camera installations, the Air Force settled on a camera fit for the U-2 that involved just one Hycon 73B shooting through a huge lens with a 36in focal length.

The whole 'B-camera' installation, complete with its 9.5in-wide film, weighed several hundred pounds and produced high-resolution 18in by 18in photos.

The B-camera would *not* fit inside a Q-2. So Hycon miniaturized it, reducing the focal length to 24in and shrinking the format to 9in by 9in.

Soon the Hycon 233A camera was ready. It just needed a bigger magazine to hold all 2,500ft of film Ryan Aeronautical estimated the drone would need for a deep-penetration mission. The Litton-made navigation system already worked pretty well, and it would get even better with a little refinement, Schwanhausser explained.

One of Schwanhausser's main concerns was ensuring that the drone remained 'unobserved' during its flights over enemy territory. In his technical proposal he assured the Air Force that 'the radar appearance of the modified drone will render the drone virtually undetectable, making it the least detectable existing aircraft.'

It was one thing to promise such a high degree of stealth. It was another actually to deliver on that promise. For the first phase of Red Wagon, Schwanhausser and his team ordered up scale models of the Q-2C and irradiated them at a facility on the ground.

The Ryan Aeronautical team concluded it could reduce the drone's radar signature by placing a mesh screen over the engine intake, painting the nose with non-conductive paint and blanketing the drone's sides with a sheet of radar-absorbing materials.

Flight tests came next. Ryan Aeronautical modified its four Q-2C test drones with the mesh, paint and RAM blanket and shipped them to Holloman Air Force Base in New Mexico. Before it launched the first test sortie, the company prepared a press release with a cover story, just in case a drone strayed beyond the test range and caught the public's eye.

The cover story was that Ryan Aeronautical was developing an improved target drone, the Q-2D. 'This ground-controlled target will be flying missions at near-sonic speed and at altitudes in excess of 60,000 feet,' the press release explained. 'It will fly for more than six hours while being fired at by surface-to-air missiles in the Air Force program of training against high-flying enemy aircraft.'

In any event, the test drones behaved and Ryan Aeronautical never had to fall back on the cover story. The four drones between September and October 1960 flew seventeen times over White Sands Missile Range adjacent to Holloman. The flights lasted fifty-one minutes on average.

Tracking the drones with radar sets, the testers confirmed the modified Q-2C's lower radar signature. The test flights also indicated the drones were stable enough to take clear photos.

Ryan Aeronautical and the Air Force were pleased with the test results. Schwanhausser began drawing up a proposal for a much more expansive, follow-on test program involving forty-six drones. Ryan Aeronautical believed that effort could help it to develop a new drone, the Model 136, that would be even stealthier than the Model 147, aka Q-2C.

In late 1960 Air Force Chief of Staff General Curtis LeMay, the legendary former bomber commander, proposed to spend $70 million on Red Wagon over the following budget cycle. 'We thought we had a going program,' Ryan said. Even the CIA had signalled its approval.

Then there was a presidential election.

Ground-launch was always an option for Q-2Cs and Model 147s, but the military discovered that aerial launch afforded the drone greater initial velocity without the use of add-on rocket boosters and also extended the range of the launch crew's radios. The ground-launch method outlasted aerial-launch, however. The last dedicated US military DC-130 retired in 2007. Subsequent launches of Model 147-style drones were from land or sea. (*Teledyne Ryan photo courtesy of the San Diego Air and Space Museum Archive*)

This photo montage depicts a Q-2C target drone in flight. The Q-2C was a bigger and more powerful version of the 1948-vintage Firebee. Ryan Aeronautics promoted the Firebee as a potential recon vehicle as far back as 1955 but, gaining no traction, the company abandoned the idea until shoot-downs of U-2s in the early 1960s compelled the US Air Force to look for an alternative to manned recce planes. (*Teledyne Ryan photo courtesy of the San Diego Air and Space Museum Archive*)

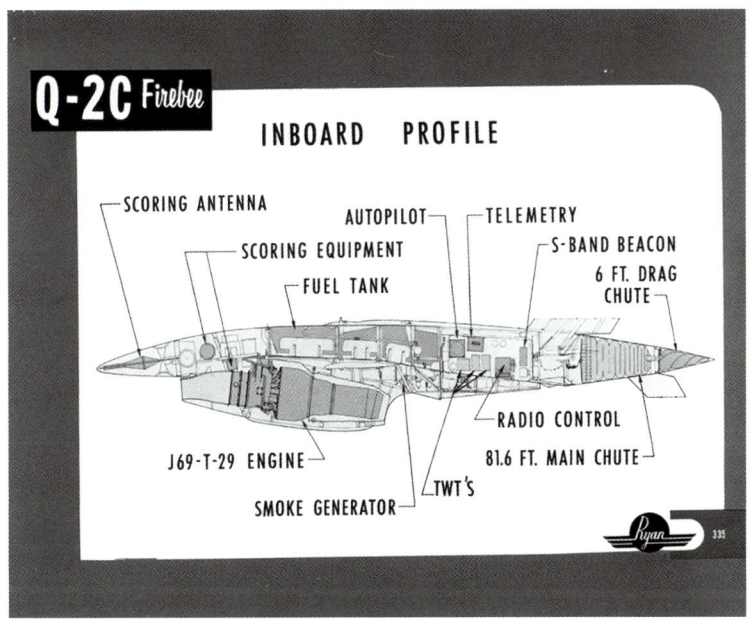

Ryan Aeronautical's Q-2C entered production in 1960. The jet-propelled, swept-wing drone – 23ft long from tip to tail – could fly as low as 50ft and as high as 60,000ft. It boasted a J69 turbojet producing 1,700lb of thrust. (*Teledyne Ryan art courtesy of the San Diego Air and Space Museum Archive*)

Launched via rocket booster from the ground or two at a time from under the wing of a mothership plane, the Q-2C could complete 'all flight maneuvers', according to Ryan Aeronautical's Bob Schwanhausser, and all while under remote control. A radar beacon on the drone helped the operators to track it. A telemetry link fed the operator vital data including engine revolutions per minute, airspeed and altitude. It was standard practice for the control team to mark the drone's flight path and altitude on an ink-plot, making corrections to hew the aircraft toward its pre-planned route. (*Teledyne Ryan art courtesy of the San Diego Air and Space Museum Archive*)

A US Air Force F-86 fighter tails a Q-2C during testing of the drone over White Sands Missile Range in New Mexico in August 1955. (*US Air Force photo*)

A US Air Force F-100 fighter flies alongside a Q-2C target drone. The 23ft-long, jet-propelled, swept-wing drone could fly as low as 50ft and as high as 60,000ft. It boasted a J69 turbojet producing 1,700lb of thrust. (*Teledyne Ryan photo courtesy of the San Diego Air and Space Museum Archive*)

Parachute-recovery was a feature of target drones dating as far back as the OQ-2, which first flew in 1939. However, the parachute model of recovery proved to be one of the major flaws of the later Q-2C target pictured here, as well as operational Model 147 recce drones. The parachute often failed to deploy on command. Even when it did, drones displayed a dangerous tendency to float away from the designated recovery zone and wind up in deep rice paddies, on steep hillsides, in thick jungles in enemy territory or even, at least once, inside the fence of a US government nuclear facility. (*Teledyne Ryan photo courtesy of the San Diego Air and Space Museum Archive*)

Q-2s played the victim in air-combat training for four decades ending in the 1980s. The target drone outlasted many of the fighter types that pursued it. Pictured here is a very early Q-2 with F-102s from several squadrons including, closest to the drone, the 318th Fighter-Interceptor Squadron, which flew the supersonic F-102 from McChord Air Force Base in Washington State between 1957 and 1960. Captain Norman Burzynski from the 112th Fighter Group in a 1963 magazine article called the Q-2 the 'common enemy' of US Air Force interceptor squadrons. (*Teledyne Ryan photo courtesy of the San Diego Air and Space Museum Archive*)

To fit the U-2 manned spy plane's Model 233 camera into the Model 147 spy drone, camera-maker Hycon miniaturized it, reducing the focal length to 24in and shrinking the format to 9in by 9in. The Hycon 233A also needed a bigger magazine to hold all 2,500ft of film Ryan Aeronautical estimated a drone would need for a deep-penetration mission. (*Hycon photo*)

**HR-233** HIGH ALTITUDE AERIAL RECONNAISSANCE CAMERA

FORMAT 9 x 9 INCHES
f8 - 24 INCH FOCAL LENGTH LENS,
FOLDED OPTICAL PATH
790 FT THIN BASE FILM

VIEW ANGLE 90° - THROUGH
VARIABLE FIVE POSITION MODE
FMC - ROCKING MOUNT
HIGH RESOLUTION

There were lots of ways to launch Q-2C target drones, and the same methods worked for operational Model 147 recce drones. Ground-launch was simplest but required a drop-away rocket booster that helped to accelerate the drone to cruising speed. For aerial launch, a mothership plane – the C-130 cargo plane was the most popular – effectively functioned as the booster, with the added bonus of hauling the unmanned vehicle to cruising altitude before launch. (*Teledyne Ryan photo courtesy of the San Diego Air and Space Museum Archive*)

The US Air Force and US Navy adapted a wide range of aircraft types to function as motherships for Q-2 target drones and, later, operational Model 147 drones. Air Force B-26 medium bombers launched Q-2s during developmental testing of the type in 1952 and 1953. By the mid-1960s the Air Force had settled on the C-130 airlifter as the basis of its main mothership type, while the Navy used DP-2 motherships based on the P-2 maritime patrol plane. (*Routine aerial launch of Ryan Aeronautical Teledyne Ryan art courtesy of the San Diego Air and Space Museum Archive*)

A Q-2 target drone target launches from its US Air Force B-26 mothership during developmental testing of the drone over Holloman Air Force Base in New Mexico in 1952 or 1953. (*Teledyne Ryan photo courtesy of the San Diego Air and Space Museum Archive*)

The two oldest DC-130 motherships, serials 57-0496 and 57-0497, could carry as many as four Q-2Cs at a time, but for front-line recce missions all DC-130s carried just two Model 147s, with one of the drones functioning as a back-up for the primary aircraft. DC-130s 496 and 497 received their mothership modifications while still on the Lockheed production line. They went straight to the US Air Force's Missile Development Center at Holloman Air Force Base in New Mexico. There they supported development of the Model 147 and also launched the first Model 147B reconnaissance missions over China. These oldest DC-130s eventually transferred to the US Navy. (*Teledyne Ryan photo courtesy of the San Diego Air and Space Museum Archive*)

A US Navy H-34 helicopter from Squadron VC-8 carries one of the unit's Q-2C target drones after recovering the unmanned vehicle following a flight over the Atlantic Ocean. The Puerto Rico-based VC-8 through the 1960s operated Q-2C drones, P-2 launch planes and H-34s for drone recovery. (*Teledyne Ryan photo courtesy of the San Diego Air and Space Museum Archive*)

Ryan Aeronautical's 'Red Wagon' project launched in the summer of 1960. Courtland Perkins, the Air Force's assistant secretary for research and development, believed the program was a waste of time. Courtland phoned Lieutenant Colonel Lloyd Ryan, the US Air Force's deputy reconnaissance chief, and told him to cancel Ryan Aeronautical's study contract. Ryan didn't want to do that. He called up Ryan Aeronautical in San Diego 'to find out how far along they were,' he recalled. 'We just went ahead and did the test program.' (*Teledyne Ryan art courtesy of the San Diego Air and Space Museum Archive*)

Nose art, mission markings and nicknames were a feature of Q-2C and Model 147 drones throughout the service lives of both types. Pictured here is Q-2C 'I Go Pogo No. IV' hanging on a US Air Force B-26 mothership plane in the early 1950s. 'Tom Cat' was a Model 147SC that held the record for survivability, completing sixty-eight missions over North Vietnam before succumbing to enemy air defenses in September 1974. 'Budweiser', 'Ryan's Daughter' and 'Baby Buck' were also long-lived Model 147SCs, respectively with sixty-three, fifty-two and forty-six missions. 'Big Red' was a Model 147SC that Ryan Aeronautical modified to carry weapons around 1972. (*US Air Force photo*)

# Chapter Three

Republican Vice President Richard Nixon's loss to Democrat Senator John F. Kennedy meant a new political party would be taking over in Washington, D.C. starting in January 1961. Military policy would be in limbo until then.

On those grounds, Harold Brown, the Pentagon's top weapons-tester, nixed Red Wagon's budget. The abrupt cancellation shocked Schwanhausser. He flew to Washington, D.C. to try to save his program.

He met with Nixon, who declined to intervene on Ryan Aeronautical's behalf but did arrange for Schwanhausser to meet with outgoing defense secretary Thomas Gates, but Gates was only barely aware of the drone effort. After all, Schwanhausser recalled, just six people in the entire Defense Department had any direct involvement with Red Wagon.

Gates could have solved Schwanhausser's problem with a mere signature, but he demurred. Schwanhausser learned later that Gates had seen LeMay's $70 million budget proposal and had rejected it with a simple hand-written note that read, 'I thought we weren't going in this direction.'

'That's the way programs get stopped,' Schwanhausser grumbled. Ryan Aeronautical began firing people from Schwanhausser's staff. The company's recce drone efforts went into limbo.

Still, the modest study contract over the summer of 1960 had kept Ryan in the spy drone business for a critical period during which all those fraught predictions about U-2s getting shot down and their pilots being captured or killed tragically came true.

U-2 pilot Powers, now a prisoner of the Soviets, was a living – and, for the Americans, embarrassing – reminder of the U-2's vulnerability to modern air defenses.

On May 5, 1960, four days after Powers' shoot-down, Soviet premier Khrushchev publicly announced that Soviet forces had downed an American spy plane. The Eisenhower administration, initially believing that Powers had died in his plane's destruction, at first tried to obfuscate the true nature of the fateful U-2 mission.

American officials claimed an 'unarmed weather research plane' belonging to the National Aeronautics and Space Administration had been conducting a routine weather-reconnaissance flight in Turkish airspace when it had suffered a malfunction in its on-board oxygen system.

Powers had blacked out, the Americans explained. With its pilot incapacitated, the 'weather plane' had veered into Soviet airspace by accident. 'The United States government requests the Soviet government to provide it with full facts of the Soviet investigation of this incident,' the US State Department stated in a diplomatic cable.

Two days later Khrushchev revealed that Powers was alive. What's more, Soviet inspectors had examined the U-2's wreckage and confirmed that it was indeed a spy plane carrying powerful cameras and other sensitive equipment. 'The American aircraft intruded across the borders of the Soviet Union for aggressive reconnaissance purposes,' Soviet officials explained in a diplomatic cable.

The Eisenhower administration panicked. Secretary of State Christian Herter even tried to blame the Soviets for Powers' mission. The Soviet Union's own refusal to reveal details of its nuclear arsenal forced the United States to conduct secret overflights, Herter claimed.

'The government of the United States would be derelict to its responsibility not only to the American people but to free peoples everywhere if it did not, in the absence of Soviet co-operation, take such measures as are possible unilaterally to lessen and to overcome this danger of surprise attack,' Herter stated.

Eisenhower refused to rule out future overflights. 'It is a distasteful but vital necessity,' the president said during a May 11 news conference. Incensed, Khrushchev and his delegation abruptly walked out of a diplomatic summit in Paris on May 17.

Yet Eisenhower's public defiance masked secret uncertainty. After Powers disappeared, the CIA quickly recalled all of its overseas U-2 detachments. The military and the CIA added new layers of approvals for any dangerous aerial spying missions, and Eisenhower imposed a moratorium on spy missions over the Soviet Union. Eisenhower's successor Kennedy extended the moratorium.

It was becoming US policy that it was too risky to send manned spy planes into the most heavily-defended and politically sensitive airspace. That policy held even when, in February 1962, the Powers debacle finally came to an end.

The Americans and Soviets agreed to an exchange: Gary Powers for Rudolf Abel, a Soviet spy the Federal Bureau of Investigations had nabbed back in 1957. The trade went down at the Glienicke Bridge in Berlin. Before sending Powers across the so-called 'Bridge of Spies', a Soviet official addressed the pilot: 'The next time you come to see us, come as a friend.'

The White House's moratorium on spy flights over the Soviet Union did *not* apply to the territory of Soviet client states. Nor did it apply to any U-2s that America's allies might operate.

So in 1959 the United States began supplying the Taiwanese Air Force with U-2s, as well as all the training, logistical and intelligence support the island country might require in order to operate the high-flying planes.

Taiwanese U-2s flew missions over eastern China's main industrial and population centers starting in 1962. CIA-operated U-2s didn't totally avoid China. Taking off from India and Pakistan, American U-2s periodically probed nuclear test sites in sparsely-populated western China.

Yet the Taiwanese U-2s were in the thick of it. They flew in broad daylight within full view of Chinese interceptors. Han Decai, a Chinese Air Force MiG-17 pilot, described his frustration to CIA historian Bob Bergin. 'We did our best to attack them, but the problem was the extreme altitude at which the U-2 flew,' Han said. 'We could not reach them.'

However, the S-75 *could* reach them. Chinese S-75s shot down their first Taiwanese U-2 on September 9, 1962. By the time the Taiwanese U-2 program folded in 1974, the island's air force had lost no fewer than eleven U-2s. Chinese S-75s accounted for most of the kills.

Taiwan's losses loomed over the CIA's U-2 force as it eyed a new target: Cuba. In 1960 rumors circulated in Florida's Cuban-American community that the Soviet Union was arming the regime of Cuban dictator Fidel Castro. Agency U-2s began flying over Cuba in October 1960, their first missions since Powers' shoot-down. CIA pilots fell into a rhythm of twice-a-month missions over the island.

In early 1962 Khrushchev, frustrated by the slow progress of the Soviet Union's efforts to develop reliable ICBMs, ordered the Kremlin to deploy R-14 nuclear-tipped medium-range ballistic missiles to Cuba. Soviet technicians also installed 144 S-75 launchers.

The S-75s were a sure sign that the Soviets were protecting something important in Cuba. The CIA spotted the air-defense missiles *before* it detected the nukes. A U-2 photographed S-75 sites in Cuba on August 29, 1962. It wasn't until October 14 that one of the CIA planes spotted an R-14 missile.

China's destruction of a Taiwanese U-2 that September startled the Americans, but didn't totally deter them from continuing the missions over Cuba. Indeed, the White House's growing concern over the Cuban situation compelled it to *loosen* the approval process for U-2 overflights.

General Lieutenant S.N. Grechko, commander of the Soviet S-75s in Cuba, was under strict orders to fire his missiles only in the event of open warfare with the Americans. The restrictions rankled Castro, who in late October 1962 ordered his own forces to open fire on American planes. Cuban air-defense guns couldn't reach the high-flying U-2s, but all the shooting along with a tightening US naval blockade helped to contribute to a deepening sense of impending doom.

Convinced that war was inevitable, on October 27 Grechko ordered his troops to target a U-2 flying near Victoria de las Tunas. Three V-750s struck the U-2, killing US Air Force Major Rudolph Anderson. This shoot-down, perhaps more than any event in world history, almost triggered a civilization-ending nuclear war.

The Americans were in shock. Even Khrushchev realized his forces had overstepped the mark. 'You were hasty,' the Soviet leader cabled to Grechko. Fortunately for all life on Earth, diplomacy over the following days helped to defuse the crisis. The Soviets withdrew both the R-14s *and* the S-75s from Cuba.

Meanwhile at the Pentagon, views on drones finally, and permanently, were changing. In September 1961, the Kennedy administration, acting on an initiative that originated under Eisenhower, established the National Reconnaissance Office (NRO) to oversee American spy satellites and strategic reconnaissance planes. The NRO would remain an official secret until 1995.

The agency's founding director, Joseph Charyk, swiftly consolidated Air Force, Navy and CIA space activities under his control. He also directed millions of dollars into a highly-secret fund with loose contracting rules that the NRO called 'Big Safari'.

Big Safari skirted labyrinthine spending regulations by mostly modifying existing equipment rather than developing new equipment from scratch. The idea was that Big Safari would frequently help the NRO and quickly modify surveillance gear in order to keep pace with enemy developments.

Charyk and the NRO loved drones. In February 1962 the agency tapped Big Safari rules in order to pay Ryan Aeronautical a little more than $1 million to modify four Q-2Cs into what the NRO called the Ryan Model 147A Firefly.

Building on its summer 1960 test program, Ryan Aeronautical got to work. In a ninety-one-day spasm of engineering and trials, the company built and tested the four Model 147As. In one test, a GC-130 mothership plane flying from Holloman Air Force Base in New Mexico launched a Model 147A that then flew 670 miles to the Great Salt Lake in Utah and then back to Holloman for recovery.

In another test in May 1962, Air Force F-106 interceptors tried to detect a Firefly heading straight toward them. They failed. Air Force fighters also took live missile shots at the Fireflies from behind. They missed.

The NRO was thrilled with the test results. However, the agency doesn't own much of its own infrastructure. Rather, it oversees and tasks surveillance forces that actually belong to the CIA, the Air Force and the Navy. To ensure it could tap the Model 147As for operational missions, the NRO first needed some other government agency to take ownership of the drones.

So the NRO went calling across the military bureaucracy. The general in charge of the Air Force's Tactical Air Command flatly stated that he 'wanted no part of unmanned aircraft'. Strategic Air Command was only slightly more accommodating. Several SAC offices rejected the drone.

The NRO was growing desperate when SAC's director of operations, Major General William Blanchard, saved the Model 147A from erasure. 'He accepted the system on the spot,' Ehrhard wrote. 'SAC had just bought into the most significant operational UAV system in history, one that would soon be elevated from obscurity by world events.'

In the heady hours following the 1962 U-2 shoot-down, intelligence officials frantically looked around for alternative means of gathering intel over Cuba.

The Firefly was an obvious candidate, but sporadic funding – and the abortive 1960 stop-work order from Perkins – had slowed Ryan Aeronautical's efforts to build and test the recce drones. The company had completed just two of the NRO's Fireflies by the time of the Cuban missile crisis. Flight-testing was incomplete.

However, that didn't stop Charyk from calling up the two Fireflies from their test effort in New Mexico. Ryan Aeronautical dutifully loaded the drones under the wing of their GC-130 mothership plane. The GC-130 sat on the runway at Tyndall Air Force Base in Florida, its crew waiting for the word 'go'.

Catching wind of the planned Cuba sortie, Colonel Ryan at the Pentagon flew into action. While he strongly supported Ryan Aeronautical's recce drones, he strongly *opposed* deploying them over Cuba. 'The Air Force side did not want to use drones in Cuba,' Ryan explained. 'We only had two, and we had great visions of greater potential elsewhere', that is to say saving the Fireflies for missions over the Soviet Union. If a drone got shot down over Cuba, the Soviets would know the Americans possessed a new reconnaissance capability.

Ryan found LeMay at the Pentagon and they hurried to Charyk's office. The NRO chief was in a meeting with General Thomas Powers, the head of Strategic Air Command. LeMay, himself a former SAC boss, tossed Powers out of the office. 'LeMay flat out told the undersecretary not only "No", but "Hell, no",' Ryan told historian Thomas Ehrhard for a 2010 study. The NRO canceled the Cuba mission.

The nuclear near-miss of late 1962 gave the drone program a 'badly-needed impetus', William Wagner, a former Ryan Aeronautical vice president, wrote in one of his two seminal books on the company's drone designs.

Charyk for one was only temporarily cowed by LeMay's bullying. Shortly after the Air Force strong-armed the NRO into canceling its drone mission over Cuba, the recon office under Charyk cut a $13 million contract with Ryan Aeronautical for seven modified Firefly drones. Ryan Aeronautical referred to them as 'Model 147Bs'.

With its 27ft wingspan, the Ryan Model 147B could climb to an altitude of 62,500ft, a full 10,000ft higher than the Model 147A, aka 'Q-2C', could achieve. The Model 147B also boasted a new navigation system and a contrail suppressor.

Demand for Fireflies continued to grow, as did the drones' sophistication. Around the same time that the NRO was ordering up Model 147Bs, the CIA asked Ryan Aeronautical to develop a version of the Firefly specifically for spying on Soviet S-75 missile batteries in Cuba. The agency gave the effort the code-name 'Long Arm'.

The resulting Model 147D borrowed the airframe of older Model 147Cs so it had the C's 15ft-span wing. That meant it couldn't fly as high as the Model 147B, but it boasted a unique set of radar receivers that could detect the various signals traveling in and around S-75 batteries.

'This not only included picking up the radar tracking frequencies, but also characterizing the terminal tracking and warhead arming and fuzing signals,' Ehrhard noted. The drone relayed the intel via radio data-link to specially-outfitted RB-47s.

That relay was important, especially when it came to capturing the V-750 missile's fuzing signal. The V-750 boasted a radio proximity fuze, basically a tiny, quick-pulsing radar packed alongside radar receivers in the missile's nose cone.

As the V-750 arced toward its target at three-and-a-half times the speed of sound, the fuze 'listened' for the return signal from the target plane. A ping from the target meant the missile was close enough for its 478lb warhead to inflict lethal damage. The fuze triggered the warhead. The whole process took a fifth of a second.

The CIA already had a rough sense of how the S-75 worked. Carefully studying photos of the air-defense system from military parades in Moscow, agency analysts actually built their own S-75s, or rough approximations at least. Live tests of the ersatz S-75s clued the military in to evasive tactics. A hard turn, for instance, could help a pilot to out-maneuver incoming V-750s.

The reconstructions didn't duplicate the V-750 missile's 5E11 Shmel-model fuze, but the CIA understood the fuze's basic design thanks to an S-75 operator's manual the agency had acquired. The agency hoped to pass along the data to the military so that it could develop countermeasures to the S-75.

Still, the CIA wasn't entirely confident in its English translation of the manual. Some of the finer technical points of the S-75's operation remained a mystery. One of the agency's goals with the Long Arm Model 147D was to determine the exact frequency of the V-750's fuzing signal … by sending a drone on a suicide mission.

The plan was for a Firefly to offer itself to a Soviet S-75 battery in Cuba. Radar receivers on the drone would capture the fuzing signal of the V-750 missiles streaking in for the kill. The drone would relay the fuzing-signal data to the nearby RB-47 in the instant before the V-750s detonated and destroyed the drone.

To ensure the S-75s opened fire, Ryan Aeronautical fitted the Model 147Ds with radar reflectors, increasing their radar signatures. Unmodified Fireflies without the reflectors were just too stealthy to make good bait.

Ryan Aeronautical tweaked three earlier Fireflies into Model 147Ds. The variant was operational by December 1962, precisely the time the Soviets began standing down their S-75 batteries in Cuba. The CIA's missile-hunting Model 147D Fireflies never saw action.

The agency for a while stored the Long Arm Model 147Ds at Eglin Air Force Base in Florida. Ryan Aeronautical eventually restored the Model 147Ds to their recce configuration.

However, the CIA hadn't lost interest in the S-75 and its proximity fuze. Talk of war in Vietnam only piqued the agency's, and the military's, interest. In October 1963, Air Force headquarters directed Strategic Air Command to develop tactics for a new Long Arm drone.

The revived Long Arm effort required a new drone. Ryan added the electronic-intelligence gear from the Model 147D to the long-wing Model 147B, resulting in a new, higher-flying missile-hunter the company called the Model 147E.

By then the Model 147 had a new nickname. Someone had leaked the name 'Firefly', so the military and intelligence community gave the latest recce Model 147s a new name. From 1963 on, they were Lightning Bugs.

Chinese S-75s were plucking Taiwanese U-2 spy planes from the sky at an alarming rate when, in 1962, Lockheed designer Kelly Johnson traveled to Washington, D.C. to pitch the concept that would become the D-21 supersonic recce drone. The wreckage of the Taiwanese U-2C number 6-6691 is on display at the Military Museum of the Chinese People's Revolution in Beijing. (*Ben Wong photo*)

As part of a proxy spying effort targeting the Communist Bloc, the United States equipped the Taiwanese military with high-altitude spy planes including RB-57s and U-2s. Taiwanese U-2s flew missions over eastern China's main industrial and population centers starting in 1962. Chinese S-75s shot down their first Taiwanese U-2 on September 9, 1962. By the time the Taiwanese U-2 program folded in 1974, the island's air force had lost no fewer than eleven U-2s. Chinese S-75s accounted for most of the kills.

To transform an aerial target into an operational recce drone, Ryan Aeronautical wanted to expand the Q-2C's flying range to at least 1,100 miles in order to allow the drone to complete 'deep penetrations into the Soviet bloc', Ryan Aeronautical's Bob Schwanhausser explained. That meant adding 60 gallons of fuel capacity to the basic Q-2C, and for missions over distances of 2,500 miles, Ryan Aeronautical should develop a new version of the Q-2 with a bigger wing and a new version of the J69 engine producing 2,400lb of thrust, Schwanhausser advised. The recommendations fed into the development of the Model 147. (*Teledyne Ryan photo courtesy of the San Diego Air and Space Museum Archive*)

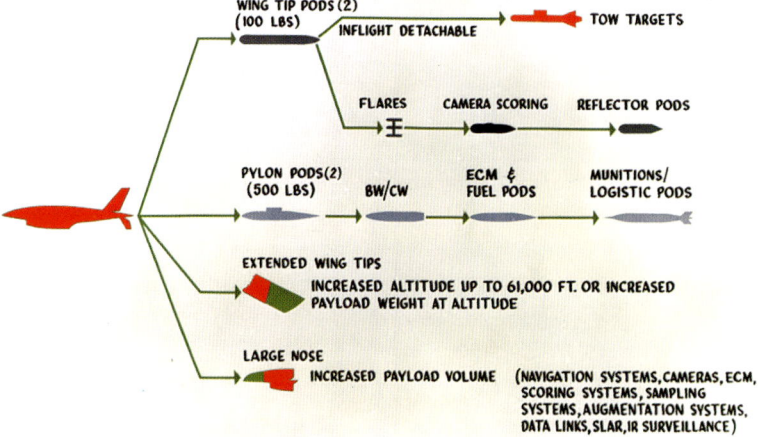

The basic Model 147 design lent itself to a wide array of modifications. (*Teledyne Ryan art courtesy of the San Diego Air and Space Museum Archive*)

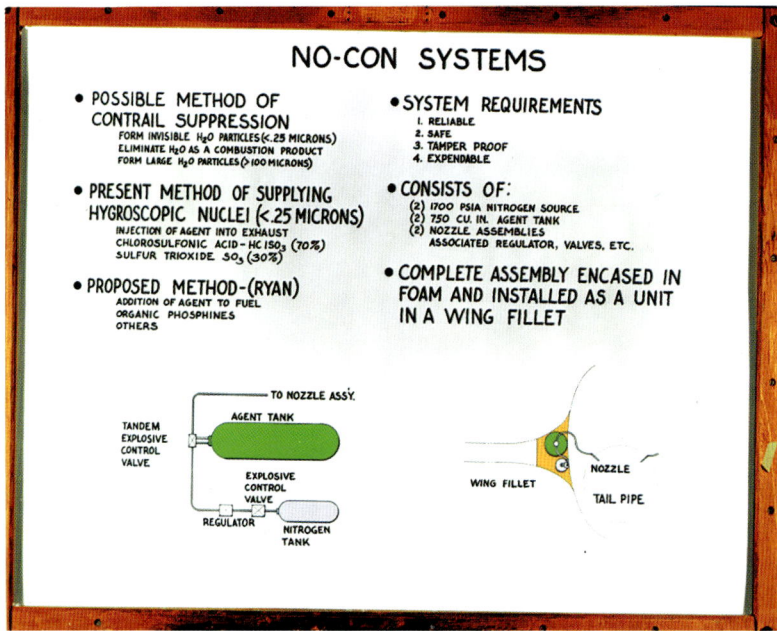

With its 27ft wingspan, the Model 147B could climb to an altitude of 62,500ft, a full 10,000ft higher than what the Model 147A, aka 'Q-2C', could achieve. Flying at that high altitude tended to produce contrails that could give away the drone's position. So Ryan Aeronautical developed a contrail-suppression system that injected a chemical agent into the drone's engine exhaust. (*Teledyne Ryan photo courtesy of the San Diego Air and Space Museum Archive*)

Teledyne Ryan's drone products through the late 1970s included dozens of variants of the Model 147. In eleven years of operations in South-East Asia, thousands of Model 147s conducted 3,435 sorties. Over the course of the war, the Model 147 evolved from a 27ft-long vehicle with a 13ft-span wing and a 1,700lb-thrust engine to a 30ft-long vehicle with a 32ft wing and an engine producing 2,800lb of thrust. (*Teledyne Ryan art courtesy of the San Diego Air and Space Museum Archive*)

Robert Schwanhausser studied aeronautics at the Massachusetts Institute of Technology, and then joined the Air Force. Few people realized that Schwanhausser actually identified as a woman and sometimes wore women's clothes while in the privacy of his own home. A life of secrecy may have contributed to Schwanhausser's high stress levels, heavy drinking and drug use. He suffered a heart attack in 1968 and nine years later nearly died of an overdose of alcohol and lithium. Schwanhausser married and divorced three times. In 2003 at the age of 72, Schwanhausser traveled to Thailand for gender-reassignment surgery. She returned home to Michigan as Bobbi Swan and died fifteen years later. (*Photo via LinkedIn*)

# Chapter Four

Ryan Aeronautical built three of the Model 147Es and was about to deliver them to the Air Force when, in January 1964, the Joint Chiefs of Staff ordered the Air Force to freeze the Long Arm effort. Like the Model 147Ds before them, the Model 147Es went into storage.

The freeze didn't last long. Vietnam was heating up, and in early 1965 SAC chief General Thomas Power asked for Air Force headquarters at least to let him have the Long Arm Model 147E Lightning Bugs and their RB-47 relay planes.

The Air Force asked the joint chiefs for permission. Not only did the service chiefs approve the request, they in turn asked the Air Force to draw up a plan to deploy the Long Arm drones to South-East Asia.

SAC got to work trialing the new drones. Three months later, the command was ready to send the Model 147Es overseas.

Politics and then circumstances repeatedly frustrated efforts by drone advocates to send Firebees and Fireflies into action. Vietnam changed everything.

On August 2, 1964, North Vietnamese torpedo boats attacked the US Navy destroyer USS *Maddox* in the Gulf of Tonkin, an arm of the South China Sea bordering Vietnam and China. The administration of President Lyndon Johnson claimed there was a second attack on August 4.

On the basis of that purported aggression by Communist North Vietnam, the White House ordered retaliatory air-raids and from Congress authorization for a wider US war effort in South-East Asia. The Vietnam War ultimately would involve half a million American Army forces fighting not only in North and South Vietnam, but also in neighboring Cambodia and Laos. It ended in American retreat in April 1975.

Some 58,220 Americans died in the war. So did more than 3 million Vietnamese. Thousands of combatants from countries supporting South Vietnam also perished, as did 1 million Cambodians in the bloody aftermath of the military conflict.

The war was a disaster for the United States, Vietnam and the whole region; a disaster that even its architects could foresee. 'Like giving cobalt treatment to a terminal cancer case, I think a long protracted war will disclose our weakness, not our strength,' Deputy Secretary of State George Ball warned Johnson in July 1965.

Yet after decades of escalating conflict between the two Vietnams and, indirectly, their respective sponsors – the Chinese and Soviets aiding the Vietnamese communists and France, the United States and other Western states backing what would become South Vietnam – Johnson and his administration were still determined to fight, and win, the war.

'I am not going to lose Vietnam,' Johnson declared shortly after Kennedy's November 22, 1963 assassination and Johnson's emergency inauguration later the same day. 'I am not going to be the president who saw South-East Asia go the way China went,' Johnson added, referring to mainland China's takeover by communist forces in 1949.

Johnson wasn't above lying to justify America's intervention in Vietnam. There's no dispute that on August 2, 1964, three North Vietnamese torpedo-boats attacked *Maddox*.

The North Vietnamese forces launched torpedoes and fired guns. *Maddox*'s crew responded with gunfire. US Navy F-8 fighters from the nearby aircraft carrier USS *Ticonderoga* strafed the torpedo-boats. No Americans were hurt. Four North Vietnamese sailors died.

The context of the skirmish is important. *Maddox* was part of an intelligence-gathering operation with the code-name 'Desoto' that began in 1962. Destroyers assigned to Desoto sailed with a van lashed to their deck. Inside the van was gear for intercepting North Vietnamese signals. The warships would sail as close as 8 miles to enemy shores to locate radar installations and listen in on communications.

The North Vietnamese were well aware of the Desoto missions and occasionally sortied a vessel of their own to shadow the American snoop. However, there was a parallel US intelligence effort about which the communist regime was not so sanguine. Under the auspices of the secret Oplan 34A, the United States deployed South Vietnamese Commandos ashore in coastal North Vietnam.

The Commandos attacked North Vietnamese coastal installations and, increasingly, drew an aggressive response from communist authorities. By July 1964 North Vietnamese troops were actively pursuing South Vietnamese infiltrators.

It had been Pentagon policy for Desoto and Oplan 34A to avoid each other. While a Commando raid was under way, the Desoto destroyers would give the area a wide berth, but communication between the two operations' respective planners broke down. *Maddox* sailed into the Gulf of Tonkin shortly after Oplan 34A raids targeting Hanoi's forces on the island of Hon Me, which lay directly off the North Vietnamese coast deep inside the gulf.

The US National Security Agency, which coordinated the Desoto signals-gathering, warned the military that the North Vietnamese might resist *Maddox*'s mission, but the warning didn't reach the destroyer itself. American provocation and incompetence were as much to blame for the Gulf of Tonkin skirmish as was North Vietnamese aggression.

In the minds of everyday Americans, as well as of the lawmakers Johnson was so eager to win to his side, the August 2 exchange of gunfire might not have been enough to justify a wider US intervention in Vietnam, but then on August 4, Hanoi's forces again attacked *Maddox*.

At least, that's what Johnson claimed in a 1971 op-ed in the *New York Times*. 'Enemy vessels were closing in at high speed,' he wrote. 'Within an hour the destroyers advised that they were being attacked by torpedoes and were firing on the enemy [patrol-torpedo] boats.'

'The unanimous view of [my] advisors was that we could not ignore this second provocation and that the attack required retaliation,' Johnson continued. 'I agreed. We decided on air strikes against North Vietnamese P.T. boats and their bases plus a strike on one oil depot.'

The retaliatory air-raids on August 5, 1964 marked the beginning of the full-scale US war in Vietnam. Johnson sought, and received on August 7, approval from Congress 'to take any measures he believed were necessary to retaliate and to promote the maintenance of international peace and security in South-East Asia,' according to the State Department's Office of the Historian.

In fact, there was no second attack, NSA historian Robert Hanyok confirmed in a 2001 article in the agency's classified journal *Cryptologic Quarterly*. In response to media pressure, the NSA in 2005 declassified the article.

The Pentagon reported the August 4 attack on the basis of NSA signals intelligence that senior officials claimed pointed to North Vietnamese naval activity in the Gulf of Tonkin. In fact, NSA officials 'mishandled' the intelligence, Hanyok explained. 'The overwhelming body of reports, if used, would have told the story that no attack occurred.'

However, Hanyok's disclosure came thirty-seven years too late. The lie worked. Johnson and the Pentagon got their war, and they'd need drones to fight it.

Ryan Aeronautical added the electronic intelligence gear from the Model 147D to the long-wing Model 147B, resulting in a new, higher-flying drone the company called the Model 147E. The company built three of the Model 147Es for the Long Arm project, which aimed to acquire vital intelligence on the deadly S-75 missile system. Ryan Aeronautical was about to deliver the Model 147Es to the Air Force when, in January 1964, the Joint Chiefs of Staff ordered the Air Force to freeze the Long Arm effort. The Model 147Es went into storage for a year. In early 1965, with aircraft losses mounting over North Vietnam, the Air Force released the Model 147Es to Strategic Air Command. (*Teledyne Ryan photo courtesy of the San Diego Air and Space Museum Archive*)

RB-47 electronic warfare planes like the one in this official photo played a key role in the four-year effort starting in 1962 to capture data on the V-750's fuze. Model 147D and E Lightning Bugs carrying special radar receivers teased S-75 batteries and attempted to relay to nearby RB-47s and EB-66s the fuze signal from an incoming V-750 in the instant before the missile exploded, destroying the drone. Five Model 147s flew as part of the Long Arm effort in 1965 and '66. The fifth and last drone finally captured the fuzing signal. Eugene Fubini, the assistant secretary of defense for research and engineering at the time, described the ultimate Long Arm mission in February 1966 as 'the most significant contribution to electronic reconnaissance in the last twenty years.' (*US Air Force photo*)

A sailor aboard USS *Maddox* snapped this photo of three North Vietnamese motor torpedo-boats in the Gulf of Tonkin on August 2, 1964. The North Vietnamese forces launched torpedoes and fired guns. *Maddox*'s crew responded with gunfire. US Navy F-8 fighters from the nearby aircraft carrier USS *Ticonderoga* strafed the torpedo-boats. No Americans were hurt. Four North Vietnamese sailors died. (*US Navy photo*)

# Chapter Five

In 1917, Ohio inventor Charles Kettering created arguably the world's first drone aircraft. The Kettering Aerial Torpedo, which the inventor nicknamed 'the Bug', launched from a dolly that ran along a portable track.

Pre-set internal pneumatic systems stabilized the Bug and kept it flying toward its target. It was, it should go without saying, crude. The operator actually had no direct control over the drone. Before launch, he estimated the distance to the target and the likely speed of the aircraft and guessed the flight time to place the drone in the vicinity of the target.

In theory a Bug could fly as far as 75 miles at a top speed of 120 miles per hour. A timer shut off the Bug's engine. The idea was that the drone would crash into the ground close enough to the target for its 180lb warhead to inflict some damage.

The Dayton-Wright Airplane Company built around fifty Bugs before the end of the Great War, but none of the rudimentary drones saw combat, and in the years following the war the US Army quickly lost interest.

However, drones endured … as toys. With the advent of small gasoline engines in the 1930s, radio-controlled scale airplanes went mainstream. British-born actor Reginald Denny was at home in Hollywood when he heard a loud noise coming from next door. He went to investigate and found his neighbor's son tinkering with a radio-controlled toy plane.

Denny was fascinated. He launched a new business: the Radioplane Company. A chance meeting between Denny and a US Army Air Corps general led to a major production contract. During the Second World War, Radioplane built no fewer than 15,000 copies of its OQ-2 and OQ-3 for the Army and US Navy to use as targets.

An Army photographer named David Conover was visiting Radioplane's factory at the Van Nuys Airport in Los Angeles in June 1945 when he noticed a particularly gorgeous young worker. Conover snapped a photo of Norma Jeane Dougherty (née Mortenson) holding a drone propeller. The picture ran in *Yank, the Army Weekly*, launching a film career for Dougherty under the screen name Marilyn Monroe.

The 100lb OQ-2 boasted a two-cylinder, six-horsepower piston engine spinning contra-rotating propellers for a maximum speed of around 85 miles per hour. The operator launched the drone via catapult and steered it via radio using a simple joystick. If the drone managed to avoid destruction, it could pop a parachute and float back to the ground for re-use.

Target drones were common during the Second World War. Both sides in the conflict applied the same technology to front-line weaponry including rudimentary guided bombs and, more tragically, explosives-laden, radio-controlled bombers.

In some cases, on-board crews controlled the drone bombers from take-off until cruising altitude, then bailed out. Joseph Kennedy, Jr, brother of the future US president, died in 1944 when one of the Navy's drone B-24s exploded prematurely.

After the war, the US military ratcheted back the riskier drone programs but continued buying simple flying targets. Some of those target-drones evolved into front-line systems. The OQ-2 that Norma Jeane Dougherty built became the SD-1 Falconer.

The SD-1 launched from a ramp, with twin rocket-boosters lending it the airspeed it needed to achieve lift. Propelled by a 72-horsepower piston engine, the Falconer could fly as far as 100 miles from its controller at a top speed of 185 miles per hour. For recovery, it flew home and popped a parachute.

The Falconer carried a KS-54 or KS-61 camera. The drone control unit – around a dozen soldiers riding in jeeps and trucks hauling drones, ramps, radios and a simple, short-range radar set – practised quickly setting up and packing up in order to keep pace with fast-moving troop columns.

The Army acquired around 1,500 SD-1s starting in 1959. The last Falconer unit disbanded in the mid-1970s, by which time the piston-powered drone was hopelessly obsolete.

A breakthrough occurred in 1948, when Ryan Aeronautical became the first company to mate a jet engine with a radio-controlled airframe.

'Use of the jet engine vastly increased the performance envelopes in both speed and altitude, providing aerial targets which could match – or even exceed – the capabilities of the fighter aircraft shooting against them,' Schwanhausser explained in his early-1960 presentation at the Pentagon.

Jet engines were one huge advancement for drones. Better electronics were another. 'The refinement of electronic systems within the drone, coupled with more efficient radar tracking systems, extended the range of the targets from a few miles to 50 – from 50 to 100 – and eventually ranges up to 200 miles, under remote control,' Schwanhausser continued.

Ryan Aeronautical's Q-2C, which was brand-new in 1960, built on these advancements. The jet-propelled, swept-wing drone – 23ft long from tip to tail – could fly as low as 50ft and as high as 60,000ft. It boasted a J69 turbojet producing 1,700lb of thrust.

Launched via rocket booster from the ground or two at a time from under the wing of a mothership plane, the Q-2C could complete 'all flight maneuvers', according to Schwanhausser, and all while under remote control.

A radar beacon on the drone helped the operators to track it. A telemetry link fed the operator vital data including engine revolutions per minute, airspeed and altitude. It was standard practice for the control team to mark the drone's flight path and altitude on an ink-plot, making corrections to hew the aircraft toward its pre-planned route.

At a cost of around $100,000 per vehicle in 1962, the Q-2C in theory was expendable. Fighter crews could expend live ammunition as they pursued the speedy drones, but if the Q-2C evaded destruction, it could pop its twin parachutes and safely descend back to Earth. Landing in the conventional fashion was out of the question. Ryan Aeronautical omitted landing gear from the Q-2 design in order to save weight.

As the Q-2C evolved into an operational reconnaissance craft, its size, weight and complexity inevitably grew. Arguably the most important addition was an inertial navigation system.

Q-2C target drones could broadcast their position by way of a radar beacon, ensuring that controllers on the ground always knew where they were and could confidently send course corrections via radio. What's more, a target drone rarely flew more than 200 miles from its launch point.

An operational Model 147, by contrast, couldn't risk broadcasting its location lest enemy forces track it, too. Moreover, a front-line drone might need to travel hundreds of miles – more than 1,000 miles, in some cases – in order to accomplish its mission.

So a combat-capable version of the drone needed to be able to navigate on its own, reverting to remote control only when in close proximity to its air-, ground- or sea-based controller.

Inertial navigation met that need. An inertial-navigation system is in essence a self-contained set of gyroscopes and accelerometers that constantly performs a series of dead-reckoning guesses as to the vehicle's position and can activate the vehicle's control surfaces at pre-programmed times in order to execute course changes.

A gyroscope measures changes in direction. An accelerometer measures inertia; that is, speed. A magnetometer is a compass. Combine all three, and a vehicle's onboard computer can guess with some precision where the vehicle is, where it's heading and how fast it's going there.

No inertial-navigation system is perfect, and all of them rely on accurate programming. Operator error failed early navigation systems as often as the systems themselves failed their operators.

However, a 1960s-vintage inertial-navigation system such as those built by Litton drifted at a rate of just 1 mile per hour of flight time. So a three-hour mission covering 1,500 miles should, in theory, end with the drone arriving within 3 miles of its destination. In practice, the Model 147s weren't always that accurate.

US Army photographer David Conover shot this famous photo of Norma Jeane Dougherty, a worker at the Radioplane drone factory at the Van Nuys Airport in Los Angeles, for the June 1945 issue of *Yank, the Army Weekly*. The photo launched the acting career of Dougherty, who later changed her name to Marilyn Monroe.

Radioplane's OQ-3 was an upgrade of the company's OQ-2 radio-controlled target drone. Featuring a steel-tube fuselage and fabric-covered wooden wings, the drone was launched via catapult and recovered by means of a parachute. The US Army and Navy bought thousands of OQ-2s and OQ-3s during the Second World War in order to train anti-aircraft gunners. The Army briefly experimented with operational uses of the Radioplane drone family, even testing whether the OQ-3 could lay communication wires from the air. (*Pima Air and Space Museum photo*)

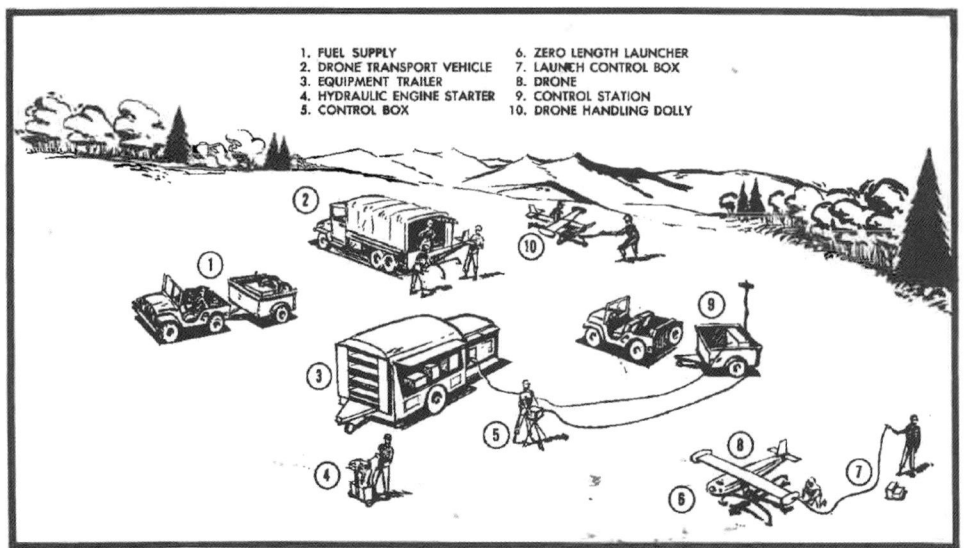

The US Army's SD-1 recce drone launched from a ramp, with a detachable rocket-booster lending it the airspeed it needed to achieve lift. Propelled by a 72-horsepower piston engine, the SD-1 could fly as far as 100 miles from its controller at a top speed of 185 miles per hour. For recovery, it flew home and popped a parachute. This official artwork depicts a typical Army drone-launch unit, circa 1961. (*US Army art*)

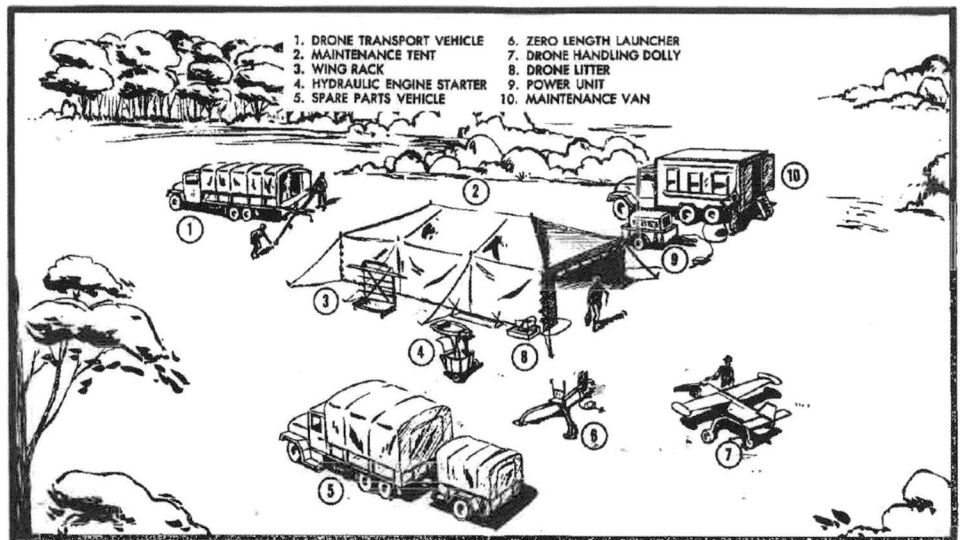

The US Army acquired around 1,500 SD-1 recce drones starting in 1959. The last SD-1 unit disbanded in the mid-1970s, by which time the piston-powered drone was hopelessly obsolete. (*US Army art*)

The US Army's SD-1 conducted short-range battlefield photographic and television surveillance. The drone launched from a lightweight stand with the aid of two rockets. A remote ground operator flew the SD-1 via radio signals and tracked it by radar. At the end of a mission, the drone floated to the ground underneath a parachute deployed from the top of the fuselage. (*US Air Force photo*)

# Chapter Six

At the time Congress signed off on the Gulf of Tonkin Resolution, Strategic Air Command's 4080th Strategic Reconnaissance Wing possessed around a dozen operational Model 147s plus their DC-130 launch planes.

The wing, which in 1963 was based at Davis-Monthan Air Force Base in Arizona, also operated U-2s. The 4080th was early to the war in South-East Asia. It set up a constellation of operating locations (OLs) across the region. President Johnson in December 1963 ordered the wing to deploy U-2s to OL 20 at Bien Hoa Air Base in South Vietnam.

The Air Force was less eager to send in the drones. 'There was a great reluctance to deploy,' Colonel Ryan told historian Wagner. 'It was due to the unknown nature of just how good it would be, and whether we would be giving away a capability that we might want to save for a bigger game.' However, there were other reasons for the internal opposition. While top Air Force brass were optimistic about the Lightning Bug's capabilities, officers at the operational level were skeptical.

'Headquarters USAF people had quite a selling job to do to get the Air Force to commit the vehicle operationally because many had serious doubts about the concept,' Fred Yochim, then an Air Force lieutenant colonel, told Wagner. Yochim, a camera specialist, had joined the drone program early on. 'There was real resistance on the part of the manned recon troops,' Yochim said.

Yochim recalled one encounter with a drone skeptic who approached the colonel after one of his presentations at the Pentagon. 'Fred, you're not really serious about this program, are you?' the skeptic asked.

'I sure am,' Yochim replied. 'Absolutely.'

'Well, it will never replace the manned reconnaissance aircraft,' the skeptic said.

'You're right, and that's the whole point,' Yochim said. 'It's not going to replace but supplement manned reconnaissance. For certain missions, it's more economical and efficient to use.'

Also safer too. Some 1,106 Ryan Aeronautical drones would fly 3,435 operational missions over South-East Asia. Almost all of the drones flew until they were shot down or crashed. A few dozen survived to return to the United States. Wagner estimated that, in substituting for manned recce planes, the drones saved the lives of 'scores' of pilots.

The Gulf of Tonkin incident shattered the Air Force's reluctance to deploy the drones. On August 4, 1964, Colonel Daniel Emrich, a deputy commander at Strategic Air Command headquarters in Omaha who was also a member of the Joint Reconnaissance Center at the Pentagon, called Ryan Aeronautical in San Diego.

Emrich told the Ryan Aeronautical drone team to get ready to deploy early the next morning. They were bound for Kadena Air Force Base in Okinawa, the southern island prefecture of Japan that functioned as the 4080th SRW's OL-8.

Air Force C-130s and C-133s would pick up the ten Ryan Aeronautical staffers in San Diego and at Eglin in Florida for the long trip to Okinawa.

The Japan base was ideal for supporting the expanding war effort in Vietnam. The idea in mid-1964 wasn't to conduct reconnaissance directly over North Vietnam, but rather to survey Chinese forces that the Pentagon feared might enter the conflict, potentially escalating the regional conflict beyond what the White House considered acceptable.

Drones would launch from Okinawa, fly west over the South China Sea between Taiwan and the Philippines, snap photos of Chinese forces on and around Hainan Island then steer east for recovery by a small detachment of technicians and helicopters operating out of Taiwan. An Air Force transport plane would speed the recovered drone back to Okinawa. After processing at a facility in Guam, the reconnaissance film would wind up at SAC headquarters in Omaha.

Conveniently, there was a Navy unit in Okinawa that launched Q-2C drones for target practice. When a Lightning Bug got a bit salty from exposure to ocean breezes or an accidental dip in the Pacific, the Air Force team could borrow Utility Squadron Five's decontamination facilities. The Lightning Bug was still highly classified and even the Q-2C operators would have no idea what the bigger drone was capable of or what it was doing in Okinawa.

The Ryan employees scrambled to put their households in order and secure spending cash from the company's financial officer. A guard at the San Diego office intercepted the employee carrying $5,000 in petty cash in a briefcase and held him at gunpoint until someone confirmed that the employee wasn't in fact robbing Ryan Aeronautical.

Airmen, contractors and crates of equipment converged on Kadena along with two DC-130s with the tail numbers 496 and 497. Inside the crates were four disassembled Model 147Bs bearing the production numbers B-8, B-9, B-10 and B-11. More drones would soon arrive.

Jack Lucast, head of the Ryan Aeronautical contingent in Okinawa, discovered that the crates lacked clear packing lists. 'We had quite a birthday party unwrapping boxes to find out what was in them,' Lucast reported back to Schwanhausser. Lucast and the other nine Ryan Aeronautical employees spent a couple days assembling the four drones. 'Experience with plastic airplane kits was helpful in uncrating and assembling new drone arrivals,' Major Thomas Doubek quipped in an official history of the 4080th SRW that the wing published in 1976.

Lucast and company finished their work just in time. Air Force meteorologists detected an incoming typhoon that they estimated might strike Okinawa with 50 miles per hour winds. Lucast and his people quickly hung the four drones on the two DC-130s and sent the mothership planes to Guam to ride out the storm. They returned three days later.

The drone detachment developed a workflow while it awaited the order to launch. In the evening, crews would hang two Lightning Bugs on one DC-130. The next workday started at 4.00 am. Crews conducted a pre-flight check on the drones and their mothership. If a launch order came, it should come between 6.00 and 8.00 in the morning.

During the pre-flight check, the Ryan Aeronautical employees and their Air Force counterparts would load the mission course into the drone's programmer. SAC provided the course weeks ahead of a planned mission in order to give the detachment time to translate a map plot into a series of timed flight events.

The programming involved one team patching into the drone, flipping switches and pressing buttons to program the vehicle's circuits while a second team checked the work of the first. This two-team method helped to ensure no one input any bad data and doomed the mission.

If no order arrived, the crew would stand down the ready drones and begin preparing for the next day ... and the next window for a first launch. Preparations included painting over the US Air Force markings on the Lightning Bugs' wings with the insignia of the Taiwanese Air Force. The recovery team in Taiwan in turn would paint over the Taiwanese markings with American ones.

Taiwan and China were already at odds. It was less destabilizing for Taiwanese aircraft to overfly China than for American planes to do the same, hence the attempted ruse. However, it was all for naught, as the airmen who were responsible for the paint jobs never sanded down the markings they were about to replace. 'You can see the shape of it pretty well,' Schwanhausser reported.

Not that the markings would help, even if the painters were thorough. If a drone crashed, it wouldn't take long for any half-informed analyst to determine that it was a fully American-made vehicle. 'The problem of eliminating all identification was not as simple as you think,' Colonel Ryan explained.

Sure, the team at OL-8 could pry the manufacturer's plates off the Model 147's fuselage and engine. However, markings 'would still be on electronic components, cameras and every kind of equipment,' Colonel Ryan pointed out.

It was counterproductive to remove those markings during the manufacturing process. After all, the drone's builder and maintainers needed markings to help with assembly and repair.

Not that the markings were really the point. 'Any reputable engineer here or abroad can take a piece of equipment and tell you its origin,' Colonel Ryan said. It's for that reason that the Air Force didn't require Ryan Aeronautical to install a self-destruct system on the Model 147. An exploded drone would still obviously be an American exploded drone.

As the 4080th SRW team at OL-8 waited for the word 'go', they did so knowing that the enemy, and the general public, eventually would wise up to their activities. Colonel Ryan was sanguine. 'If they shoot one down and announce it publicly, don't deny it, but don't acknowledge it,' he said. 'Just reply "No comment" and sweat it out.'

The order finally came on August 20, 1964. DC-130 496 took off with B-8 and B-9 on its pylons. B-9 was the primary mission drone. B-8 was the back-up in case B-9 malfunctioned. After years of starts and stops, controversy and missed opportunities, America's first truly effective drones were finally going to war.

The DC-130 winged toward the Chinese coast. Aboard were 'blue-suit' Air Force drone operators. The Ryan Aeronautical contractors stayed back at Kadena where they remotely helped to monitor the mission. A few weeks later the line would blur between the military and civilian members of the drone operation when Ryan Aeronautical employees began flying on the DC-130 motherships.

That first mission quickly ran into a problem. The launch crew aboard the DC-130 counted down to the release point and flipped the switches to launch Lightning Bug B-9. Nothing happened. The drone remained firmly attached to the DC-130. The crew hit the emergency release switch. Still nothing. B-9 refused to budge.

The DC-130 looped around for a fresh approach. This time the crew triggered B-8. There surely were sighs of relief aboard the mothership as the drone obediently separated from its pylon. The Lightning Bug motored away toward China, eventually disappearing from American radar scopes.

As the DC-130 angled back toward Okinawa, stubborn drone B-9 suddenly changed its mind. It detached from its wing pylon. Since no one aboard the mothership had ordered the drone to fire its engine, it simply glided 24,000ft down into the Pacific Ocean. A dye packet marked its final resting place.

Now everyone waited for B-8 to come home.

A few hours later, a blip appeared on the scope of the drone detachment's radar in Taiwan. It was B-8, dutifully navigating back to its pre-programmed recovery site. The drone's high-tech Doppler navigation system obviously worked as advertised.

After autonomously flying hundreds of miles at high altitude and near-supersonic speed, B-8 was just a few miles off course.

The drone popped its parachute and floated down toward a pre-designated recovery area over Taiwan. The Model 147 included an impact sensor that was supposed to register impact with the ground and release the parachute, but on that first mission the drone landed in a soggy rice paddy. The parachute failed to disconnect. Wind picked up the 'chute, flipped B-8 upside-down and dragged it across the wet ground, inflicting major damage.

Curious civilians were gathering as an Army helicopter speeded in to pick up the drone. Lucast hopped aboard DC-130 497 at Kadena and flew to Taiwan to recover B-8. It took several hours of work to pack up and ship off the undeveloped mission film and then load the damaged drone onto the DC-130.

Crates containing more drones arrived at OL-8. Nine days after B-8's successful first mission and B-9's tragi-comic dive into the sea, SAC ordered the 4080th SRW drone detachment to launch its second mission.

Model 147B-11 successfully launched and apparently completed its mission over China. The drone appeared on the scope of the recovery team's radar in Taiwan. It looked like another successful mission for the detachment.

The recovery team signaled B-11 to pop its parachute and come home, but no parachute appeared. B-11 kept right on flying. Past the recovery team. Beyond Taiwan. Out into the vast Pacific Ocean. 'It was goodbye bird,' Lucast quipped. The detachment decided a short circuit on the drone's programmer was to blame.

Schwanhausser was in Omaha, having dinner with two SAC officers. A call interrupted the meal. Strategic Air Command was unhappy. The next morning, the command's top maintenance officer, Major General A.J. Beck, told Schwanhausser he would be lending OL-8 a combined team of Air Force and Ryan Aeronautical experts. They were going to fix the Lightning Bugs … or recommend that SAC terminate the project.

Schwanhausser volunteered to go. 'Their whole future – and the company's – was at stake,' Schwanhausser wrote about his team. The 4080th SRW commander John DesPortes 'isn't looking real kindly at this unmanned stuff right now,' Schwanhausser warned.

Beck's troubleshooting team arrived in Okinawa and launched what Schwanhausser called 'a big investigation'. He determined that the Lightning Bug team's Air Force and contract personnel simply weren't getting along. 'Classic command problems,' historian Ehrhard commented.

Ehrhard attributed the 'acrimonious' relationship in part to the Model 147's relative immaturity as an operational system. Every crash resulted in 'finger-pointing' as military and contract personnel sought to deflect blame.

Beck's investigation concluded that the Lightning Bug team might function better with a different personnel mix, one that favored uniformed airmen. There were simply too many contractors at OL-8 anyway, Schwanhausser decided. He sent home four of his employees, including Lucast. 'That was supposed to have fixed everything,' Schwanhausser said.

Things were looking up. On September 3, 1964 B-10 successfully completed the detachment's third mission, but B-13's own mission six days later was a bust. The drone was on the recovery team's scope, descending from 30,000ft toward Taiwan, when it simply ... disappeared.

September 3 was an unlucky day for the detachment. The Ryan Aeronautical team had used parts it had salvaged from B-8 to build B-6. The same day B-13 disappeared, B-6 launched without incident and sped toward China. The next time any Americans saw B-6, it was in pieces and on fire in a jungle in Laos.

The wreckage contained all the components for a complete Model 147B except for its vertical stabilizer. That led some to speculate that B-6 was the victim of ground fire, a surface-to-air missile or even an enemy fighter jet.

The Lightning Bug team at OL-8 was unhappy. In a month of front-line flying, the 4080th SRW detachment and its supporting contractors had attempted five launches. Just two missions were successful. Schwanhausser's intervention hadn't ironed out all the problems.

Not only were their drones disappearing and crashing, after weeks in Okinawa the contractors were tired. Just as they were settling into the routine of briefings, maintenance, 1.00 am wake-ups for possible missions and tense, hours-long waits for drones to return, a typhoon would threaten Okinawa and force people and drones to evacuate to Guam. That happened twice.

The contractors had expected to stay at OL-8 for a month or so, just long enough to get the detachment's airmen up to speed. A few back-to-back successful missions might have justified the Ryan Aeronautical employees declaring 'mission accomplished' and heading home, but as the Lightning Bug team struggled, the contractors' deployment got extended. Then extended again.

SAC would later admit that its airmen at OL-8 were poorly trained for their jobs supporting the drones. 'Most of our personnel out here have about as much knowledge of the Lightning Bug as when they caught them when they were kids on the farm and put them into bottles,' 4080th SRW commander DesPortes, an old-fashioned manned-recce type, told Schwanhausser.

The wing's negligence regarding its own Lightning Bug element was evident in lax security procedures. Airmen left drones out in the open without so much as tarps covering them. One contractor twice reported finding the Lightning Bugs' hangar unguarded.

Despite the tension between the Ryan Aeronautical employees and their Air Force colleagues, it still came as a shock to the drone team when SAC in mid-September 1964 abruptly ordered the Lightning Bug operation at Kadena to pack up everything and move to Bien Hoa Air Base, 20 miles north of Saigon.

Someone in the senior ranks wanted the Lightning Bugs to be closer to the action, or at least *away* from Okinawa, which was still a major hub for manned reconnaissance efforts.

The move to OL-20 in South Vietnam was a disaster for the Lightning Bug team. The quarters were just tents. Rats were thick on the muddy ground. The Air Force required everyone to get inoculated against the plague. At night the gunfire was like 'a symphony', the contractors reported. One of the DC-130s got shot up.

'We were premature in basing in South Vietnam,' Schwanhausser explained. 'They didn't welcome our guys very well. The Air Force wasn't ready either facility-wise or psychologically to introduce an unmanned recce bird into their operations. Lines of authority within the Air Force were not clearly drawn, nor was the role of the contractor. Also, the South Vietnamese government hadn't been fully briefed.'

The team was at OL-20 for just eight days before SAC sent them back to OL-8. They came back to Kadena just in time to fail. *Hard*. SAC ordered up a two-drone dual mission for September 15, 1964 but the crew aborted both launches owing to electrical malfunctions.

'Clearly we had problems,' Schwanhausser wrote. 'The system had not yet been debugged.... We knew, of course, that unless literally hundreds of events in a complex series occurred at precisely the correct instant, the missions would fail.'

On September 16, 1964, Schwanhausser arrived in Okinawa for his second troubleshooting visit. This time DesPortes was with him. It would be one of the colonel's last overseas trips before a promotion to general and a new assignment as commander of the first wing to fly the new SR-71 Blackbird spy plane. 'Colonel DesPortes certainly isn't looking real kindly at this unmanned stuff right now,' Schwanhausser wrote.

Lightning Bug drones and U-2 manned spy planes, including this example depicted taxiing in 1965, shared the facilities of the 4080th SRW at Bien Hoa Air Base near Saigon. For security reasons, U-2s rarely left their hangars. The tension between the U-2 operators and their counterparts on the drone side of the detachment began to ease in late 1965 after SAC organized a joint drone-U-2 mission over Haiphong Harbor. The U-2 pilot watched in horror as a V-750 missile destroyed the drone. 'From now on, you guys can have that mission,' the pilot told the Lightning Bug operators over drinks at the Bien Hoa Officers' Club. (*US Air Force photo*)

G/DC-130 drone-mothership planes carried two stations for launch-control officers. The US Air Force and Navy converted sixteen C-130As, Es and Hs into G/DC-130s starting around 1957. The Air Force maintained a force of two DC-130s in South-East Asia throughout the war. None were lost. A few DC-130s remained in service through the early 2000s. One, a former C-130 with the serial number 57-0497, deployed to the Middle East for the 2003 invasion of Iraq and launched Firefly drones as part of an effort to spoof Iraqi air defenses. No. 57-0497 was the oldest C-130 in US military service when it finally went into storage in 2007. (*Teledyne Ryan photo courtesy of the San Diego Air and Space Museum Archive*)

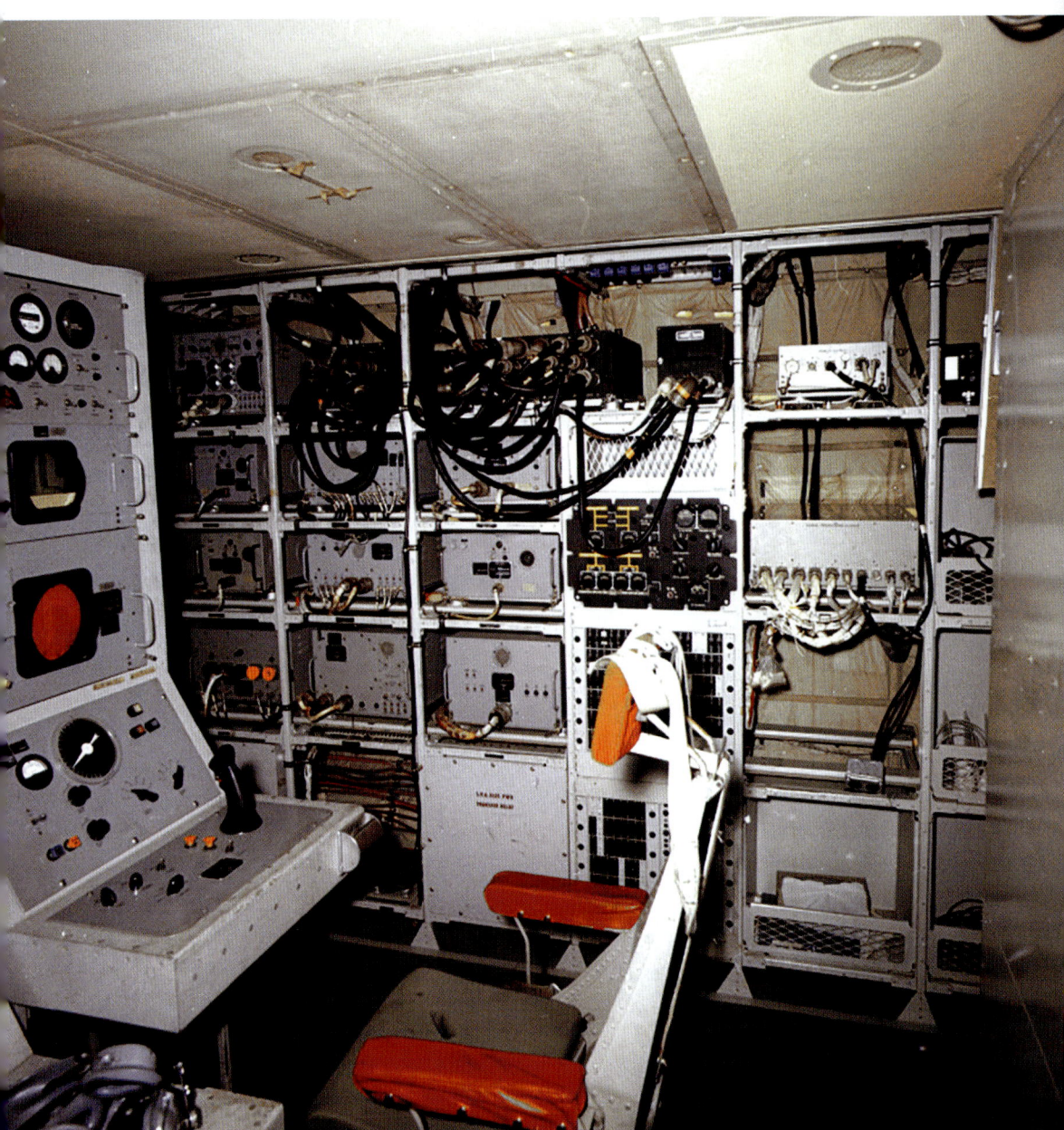

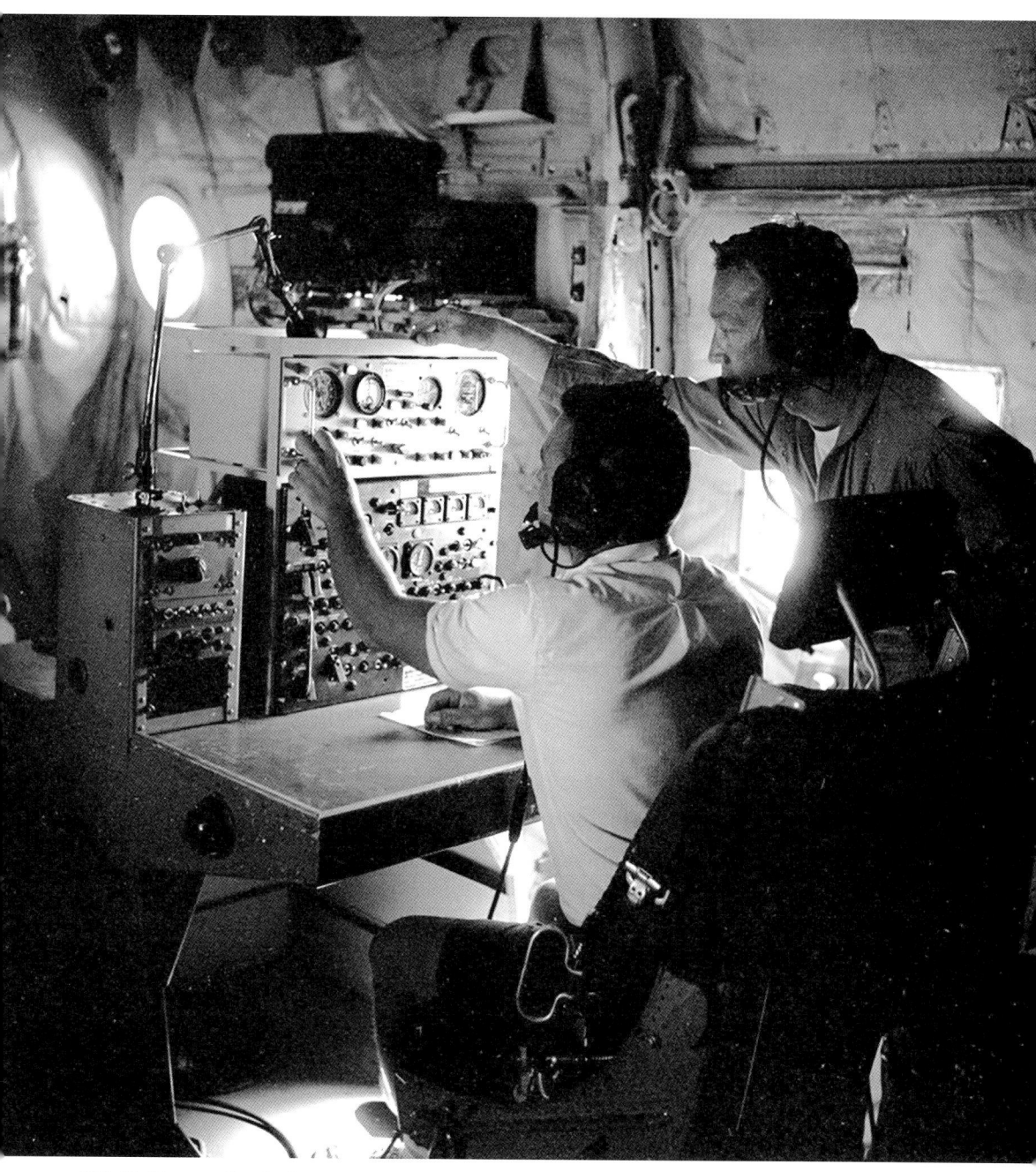

US Air Force policy in August 1964 was for 'blue-suit' Air Force drone operators to fly aboard the DC-130 mothership planes in order to launch the Lightning Bugs on their missions. The Ryan Aeronautical contractors stayed back at Kadena Air Force Base, where they remotely helped to monitor the mission. A few weeks later the line would blur between the military and civilian members of the drone operation when Ryan Aeronautical employees began flying on the DC-130 motherships, lending their greater experience to the delicate act of launching a drone. (*Teledyne Ryan photo courtesy of the San Diego Air and Space Museum Archive*)

September 3, 1964 was an unlucky day for the 4080th Strategic Reconnaissance Wing's Lightning Bug detachment. The Ryan Aeronautical team had used parts it salvaged from B-8 to build B-6. The drone launched without incident and sped toward China, but never came back. Laotian villagers eventually found B-6's wreckage in the jungle. The wreck contained all the components for a complete Model 147B except for its vertical stabilizer. That led some to speculate that B-6 was the victim of ground fire, a surface-to-air missile or even an enemy fighter jet. (*Teledyne Ryan photo courtesy of the San Diego Air and Space Museum Archive*)

US Air Force photo-interpreters such as those in this official photo carefully analyzed reconnaissance images and passed the data along to intelligence agencies and front-line combat forces. They did not, however, provide the imagery to contractors such as Ryan Aeronautical. During the early years of Ryan Aeronautical's intensive support for Model 147 drone operations, the company complained that it couldn't improve its processes if it couldn't see the results of the drones' missions and judge whether the aircraft were working as designed. (*US Air Force photo*)

After years of starts and stops, controversy and missed opportunities, America's first truly effective combat drones finally went to war on August 20, 1964. A Kadena-based DC-130 winged toward the Chinese coast. Aboard were 'blue-suit' US Air Force drone operators. That first mission quickly ran into a problem. The launch crew aboard the DC-130 counted down to the release point and flipped the switches to launch Model 147B-9. Nothing happened. The drone remained firmly attached to the DC-130. The crew hit the emergency release switch. Still nothing. B-9 refused to budge. The DC-130 looped around for a fresh approach. This time the crew triggered B-8. There surely were sighs of relief aboard the mothership as the drone obediently separated from its pylon. Pictured here are Air Force drone controllers aboard their mothership plane. (*Teledyne Ryan photo courtesy of the San Diego Air and Space Museum Archive*)

# Chapter Seven

Schwanhausser fell into the Lightning Bug team's normal routine. On mission days he awoke between 1.00 am and 1.30 am with the rest of the team. Everyone split into two groups: one to plan the mission and the other to prep the DC-130 and the two drones that were already hanging from its wings.

Programming started at 3.30 am. 'This is done with USAF people on one bird and Ryan on the other,' Schwanhausser recalled in an October 2, 1964 letter to Ryan Aeronautical president Robert Jackson.

'One man reads the program while another patches it,' Schwanhausser continued. 'Then the other two fellows change places and the patcher reads while the other checks. Then the Ryan and USAF crews exchange birds and check each other. In addition each crew has done their own planning and program calculations independently then cross-checked each other.'

On September 21, Schwanhausser personally observed one of the programmer boards go up in smoke after seventy or eighty inputs. The same malfunction could explain what happened to Model 147B-11 when it flew right past its recovery point on its fatal mission back in August.

The DC-130 took off around 7.00 am for the roughly five-hour flight to the launch point over the South China Sea. An hour later, a recovery team boarded the second DC-130 for the quick hop to Taiwan. DesPortes tended to accompany this group. 'The balance of us try to rest and grab a nap and sweat out the mission,' Schwanhausser told Jackson.

If nothing malfunctioned and no S-75s or enemy fighters intervened, the Lightning Bug came home between 2.00 pm and 3.00 pm. It took between five and eight hours to recover the drone, pack it up and fly it back to Okinawa. Meanwhile the crew at OL-8 loaded up two fresh drones for the next day's possible mission.

If SAC opted not to order up a mission, the Lightning Bug team would sleep in then head for a 10.00 am debriefing. Everyone would spend the rest of the day in the hangar maintaining the drones and the DC-130s.

It was a grueling routine. 'Each night when we go to bed we have to be prepared to awake at 1.00 am,' Schwanhausser explained. 'This certainly provides a much different set of working conditions than most of us are used to and I'm sure you can understand why these guys are tired after two months of this.'

Schwanhausser directly observed three Lightning Bug missions before penning his initial report to his boss Jackson. Wagner, in his book *Lightning Bugs and Reconnaissance Drones*, dutifully quoted Schwanhausser's observations. They underscore the difficulty in sustaining effective drone sorties.

Flight #6, Route 5021                                              Sept. 21, 1964

This bird (B-12) was dropped in a good location on time but a little to the right of the intended point. The course was about two degrees to the left of the intended course and crossed over it passing to the left. After the first leg it rolled out onto its new heading about eight nautical miles short but on a perfect heading. Approximately 120 nautical miles out, the bird turned 40 degrees to the right on a new, unexplained heading. Fortunately this was within the [control-system] limitations and control of the drone was taken.

On the initial pass over the recovery area, no command of recovery, either normal or emergency, was effective. Beacon track was also erratic and telemetry failed after one minute of operation.

[Ryan Aeronautical employee] Bill Sved convinced them [the Air Force operators] to attempt a second pass at the recovery site before heading out to sea. On the second pass, he had all recovery commands sent and the two transmitters cycled. This time, recovery was accepted by the bird and impact was on the recovery range on a knoll in winds blowing about 20 knots, gusting to 40 knots. Winds at impact area probably were 25 knots. The 'chute did not disconnect and the bird was dragged upside-down into a ravine. The nacelle broke loose and the wing and empennage were badly damaged.

This was the first flight for bird number 12. Post-flight inspection showed a faulty power supply and improperly installed parachute-release wiring. No malfunction occurred or could be found in the autopilot or programmer or rado. As a matter of fact, the bird was immediately placed on external power the next morning without any repairs despite the rough handling received the previous day. Unfortunately, the entire route had 8/8 cloud coverage and we took this flight as 'Nimbus #2'.

Flight #6, Route 5020                                              Sept. 25, 1964

This bird was dropped in a very poor launch area due to navigation difficulties in the launch aircraft. Probably no LORAN [long-range radio navigation aids] exists in this area and the C-130's Doppler [radar] was inoperative. Present information shows a good launch followed by a first leg that was two degrees to the left and ran about eight nautical miles long. The second heading was one degree to the left and 10 or 12 nautical miles short. The third heading appeared good but was soon overtaken by command control for let-down.

Recovery was normal but B-14 hit the ground moving sideways and the nacelle sheared off. This was reported by the USAF as major damage, but by cannibalizing some fittings off B-12, we had the bird back up in three normal working days. This included going into the fuel tank and resealing it. I consider this a fine job by all concerned. This was B-14's first flight.

Flight #8, Route 5021                                              Sept. 29, 1964

This drone appeared well-launched but one to two degrees left of intended heading as an average. Actually, the first 60 percent of the leg appears to be two degrees left and then changes to an almost convergent heading. The drone was 34 nautical miles long on this leg and our information shows a very slow, wide turn. The second leg commenced with about five-degree left-heading error and halfway down reduced to a two-degree error. Control was taken at that point, with the drone 19 nautical miles to the right of the intended track and recovery was very smooth and normal, requiring 25 minutes. The impact was satisfactory and damage minor, although the location prevented helicopter removal that night. This was the second flight for B-10, the first being on Sept. 3.

These missions were a mixed bag. Schwanhausser told Jackson he was pleased with the mission-planning and pre-flight checks. The process of programming the flight plans and checking the drones on both September 25 and September 29 took no longer than two and a half hours. 'It is getting to be a real smooth, clean operation.'

Schwanhausser noted that morale was improving among the Lightning Bug team's military members, thanks in large part to DesPortes' leadership.

However, Schwanhausser was unhappy with the navigation errors he observed. The Lightning Bugs too often drifted off their planned courses. It was possible to fix the error, but only with good data. Ryan Aeronautical needed to compare the Air Force's official flight plans against the courses the drones actually followed from their launch points toward China and back to Taiwan.

The data was classified. 'One of the things most needed is for us to have more access to information on actual tracks flown versus the intended routes which were programmed,' Schwanhausser explained. 'If SAC at Omaha will let us come in, with some security requirements relaxed and plot actuals versus the intended, we can do the necessary calibrating.'

The Lightning Bug's Hycon camera still wasn't working perfectly. It didn't matter if a Lightning Bug performed a flawless mission if its camera couldn't take good pictures. Schwanhausser reported that the film from the mission on September 29 was overexposed.

Perhaps the biggest risks, however, were at recovery. Drones were flying reasonably good tracks and taking acceptable pictures then crashing at the recovery range in Taiwan. 'We were having as much trouble with recovery as with anything else,' Schwanhausser recalled. 'The birds were flying pretty well and coming home, but then we'd have problems.'

The Lightning Bug had a switch that cut the cable to the parachute when it detected water, but the switch was programmed for salt water, so if a drone came down in a freshwater rice paddy, it wouldn't disconnect its 'chute. The high wind that was common at the Taiwan recovery range would drag the drone across the rough terrain, damaging it.

Still, things were looking up for the Lightning Bug team. The drones were becoming more reliable. The intelligence they gathered was increasingly useful. They were proving effective at avoiding enemy defense. 'I feel their small radar cross-section is effective against some of the SAM-site radars and I doubt if they have the capability to fuze such a weapon against us,' Schwanhausser wrote.

Similarly, the Lightning Bug's high cruising altitude appeared to prevent enemy fighter aircraft from intercepting the drones, even if the fighter pilots were capable of spotting the tiny drones. Also no one had died while supporting or operating the unmanned aircraft.

Crashes and parachute-assisted landings on difficult terrain were a feature of Model 147 testing and operations. Following the very first operational Lightning Bug mission in August 1964, Model 147B-8 popped its parachute and floated down toward a pre-designated recovery area over Taiwan. The Model 147 included an impact sensor that was supposed to register impact with the ground and release the parachute. However, on that first mission the drone landed in a soggy rice paddy. The parachute failed to disconnect. Wind picked up the 'chute, flipped B-8 upside down and dragged it across the wet ground, inflicting major damage. A Model 147T is pictured here following a 1968 landing during testing. (*Teledyne Ryan photo courtesy of the San Diego Air and Space Museum Archive*)

A wide array of US Air Force, Army, Navy and Marine Corps helicopters supporting Model 147 operations, including the heavy-lift CH-37 depicted in this photo, which apparently crashed while recovering a drone during testing in the United States. A CH-37 in October 1964 transported three airmen to recover Model 147B-14 after the drone came down in a rice paddy near Da Nang. The airmen quickly discovered that Da Nang wasn't Taiwan. Viet Cong guerrillas opened fire on the helicopter. The crew deposited the three airmen into the impact crater then flew away. A rescue force arrived soon thereafter. (*Teledyne Ryan photo courtesy of the San Diego Air and Space Museum Archive*)

# Chapter Eight

In his report to Jackson, Schwanhausser noted that 'very high-level personnel' from the Taiwanese military gathered at the recovery range to watch each time a Lightning Bug was due to return from a mission. The chief of staff of the Taiwanese armed forces personally attended each of the three recoveries Schwanhausser observed.

The Taiwanese military chief was 'very enthusiastic' about the Lightning Bugs, Schwanhausser reported, and with good reason. 'He has lost three U-2 pilots recently and likes the unmanned concept. On one flight I was told the manned aircraft was shot down immediately upon penetrating the mainland.'

It wasn't for no reason that China was working so hard to detect and shoot down the intruding U-2s. Beijing had a secret to keep. It centered on a government test site near a dried-up salt lake in Lop Nur, 1,600 miles west of Beijing. In 1959, Soviet experts had helped Chinese authorities to select Lop Nur as the site of China's future atomic bomb tests.

In the early 1960s, work at Lop Nur accelerated. US and Taiwanese leaders knew this because they were receiving regular batches of overhead imagery from Taiwan's U-2 force. Every couple of months, National Chinese pilots took off from Taiwan, winged their way through the heavy defenses of coastal eastern China and aimed their Hycon cameras at Lop Nur's facilities.

It was a dangerous duty. Between 1959 and 1971, no fewer than 10 Taiwanese U-2 pilots – more than a third of the Nationalist Chinese pilots the Americans trained – perished in accidents or during the force's 102 front-line sorties over China.

Among the dead were Yao-Hwa Chih, Huai-Sheng Chen, Te-Pei Liang, Nan-Ping Lee, Cheng-Wen Wang, Tsai-Shi Wu, Ching-Chang Yu, Jung-Bei Huang, Hsieh Chang and Chi-Hsien Huang.

Thus China's first-ever nuclear weapon test on October 16, 1964 alarmed officials in Washington but didn't surprise them. Still, the October 1964 test clearly marked the beginning of the Communist Chinese nuclear weapons program, not the end. In late '64 the Americans needed a better way to take photos of Lop Nur.

Meanwhile, the air war over Vietnam was intensifying. One solution for SAC was to try again to stage Lightning Bug flights from Bien Hoa near Saigon. Not only could Bien Hoa-based drones join the daily thrum of aerial intelligence-gathering over North Vietnam, but launching from South Vietnam also afforded the drones a path to Lop Nur that didn't take them directly over the S-75 batteries along China's south-eastern coast.

The 4080th SRW Lightning Bug detachment, including Schwanhausser and his Ryan Aeronautical team, packed up their drones and equipment and flew to Bien Hoa, settling in on the afternoon of October 8, 1964.

Three and a half hours later, the Lightning Bug detachment had loaded two drones on a DC-130 and was ready for any mission SAC might assign. However, the command signaled there would be no missions through the weekend, so on October 10 the drone detachment threw themselves what Schwanhausser described as a 'little party'.

The order to fly the following day came unexpectedly that night. 'We rousted everyone out,' Schwanhausser reported. The detachment flew three good missions over the course of a week. Then the usual gremlins got into the system.

On October 11, Model 147B-14 flew a perfect mission all the way up to recovery. The drone was 30,000ft over Da Nang when it received the radio signal from the recovery team. The Lightning Bug cut its engine and popped its parachute.

However, it was raining over the recovery zone. The drone's 'chute accumulated water and blew right off. 'Now there is a big muddy hole in the middle of a rice paddy,' Schwanhausser informed corporate headquarters.

The detachment sent three airmen in an H-37 heavy-lift helicopter to recover what they could from the rice paddy. They quickly discovered that Da Nang wasn't Taiwan. Viet Cong guerrillas opened fire on the helicopter. The crew deposited the three airmen into the impact crater then flew away.

Two HU-1 Hueys arrived, at least one of them carrying an Army Special Forces officer. The Viet Cong shot up one of the Hueys and injured the crew chief. The door gunner returned fire.

The three Ryan contractors manning the recovery van expected to have to fight their way to the crash site. 'The fellows then felt they had a fight on their hands for possession of the bird,' Schwanhausser reported.

Military personnel armed the contractors, among them Dale Weaver. 'We had been given our AR-15s and instructions on how to use them and were just getting ready to climb into the chopper when the word came back that the VC had shot up the H-37 pretty badly and that both HU-1s had engaged in a hot firefight,' Weaver wrote. 'The base commander decided to send in an Army group instead of some crazy civilians.'

A helicopter pulled everyone out of the recovery zone, temporarily leaving the site to the Viet Cong. The next day Army 'copters strafed the site, reportedly killing several Viet Cong. The drone detachment returned to the rice paddy and started digging.

It's unclear whether the Lightning Bug team ever found much of B-14 in that crater, to say nothing of recovering intact reconnaissance film. Writing as the salvage operation was under way, Schwanhausser wasn't optimistic.

That wasn't even the most disastrous drone recovery. Some months later, B-28 popped its parachute and drifted into Da Nang Bay. The Army dispatched a Huey to pick up the drone, but the helicopter broke down mid-flight and settled onto the water. The Huey's crew and the drone recovery team it was transporting, led by a 'Sgt. Goss', bailed out of the sinking chopper.

The landing-craft crew that the Navy sent to rescue the eight crash survivors found them clinging to the floating drone. A 'salty bosun's mate demanded to know how so many people got into such a little airplane,' Doubek quipped in his official history of the 4080th SRW.

The water-logged drone, B-28, flew again, and landed in water four more times. The Lightning Bug was semi-affectionately nick-named the 'Super Stupid Waterbug'.

During another recovery of a different Lightning Bug, the chopper crew lowered a soldier, laden with tools, into a rice paddy to attach a sling to the landed drone, but the crew underestimated the depth of the water. The overburdened soldier disappeared into the paddy.

A C-130 arrived from San Diego with a load of factory-fresh Model 147Bs. After B-14's dramatic loss, OL-20 launched two successful missions in late October 1964, but the detachment was still losing too many drones, in SAC's view. Schwanhausser and Weaver flew to Washington, D.C. to brief the higher-ups.

Ryan Aeronautical's Bob Reichardt, who temporarily took over from Schwanhausser at Bien Hoa, summed up the Lightning Bug operation's lingering reputational problem. 'There are still skeptics about our drones in the top Air Force levels here. They feel we sold the Air Force a bill of goods on a piece of equipment that isn't ready, and that they're being expected to meet operational standards the hardware isn't capable of achieving.'

'As you can see,' Reichardt added, 'we still have a long, hard road ahead to gain acceptance of unmanned photo reconnaissance.'

The Viet Cong almost resolved the situation themselves while Schwanhausser and Weaver were away. Moving stealthily through Saigon and across muddy fields, guerrillas closed to within a quarter-mile of the Bien Hoa perimeter and, right after midnight on November 1, 1964, peppered the flight line with almost 100 81mm mortar shells.

Terry Zimmer, an Air Force armorer, recalled the minutes leading up to the attack. 'After working our usual long day, our crew went to the airmen's club, and on our way to our hut I remember saying how quiet it was,' he told historian T.E. Bell. 'The silence changed at midnight.'

The base at the time housed two squadrons of US Air Force B-57 bombers plus an HH-43 rescue helicopter, C-47 transports, a detachment of U-2s and some South Vietnamese A-1 attack planes. Not expecting an attack and keen to be ready for the morning's missions, at night the Americans loaded up the B-57s with bombs and fuel and left them parked wingtip-to-wingtip.

It took just a few minutes of shelling to damage every single B-57 at the base and totally destroy five of them. The raid also destroyed four A-1s, two C-47s and the HH-43. Four Americans died and seventy-two were wounded. Zimmer described working overnight to haul bombs away from the burning airplane wrecks.

The attack enraged US leaders. The Joint Chiefs of Staff urged President Lyndon Johnson to retaliate with a wave of aerial bombing, but the presidential election was just two days away and Johnson wanted Americans to believe he had a handle on the war. Johnson declined to order an immediate escalation of the air war.

American reporters swarmed Bien Hoa in the aftermath of the November 1 raid. Seven months later the presence of so many reporters the previous fall would have serious ramifications for the Lightning Bug team at OL-20.

The Chinese Communist Party seized on the November attack to mock the Americans who, Chinese agents knew full well, were using Bien Hoa as a base for spy flights over China. Beijing in an official pronouncement described the raid as 'a resounding victory that shocked Washington and gladdened all the people of the world.'

Incredibly, no U-2s, Lightning Bugs or DC-130s were even damaged in the raid. No one from the 4080th SRW, military or civilian, was hurt. Reichardt, a veteran of the Second World War, found himself 'crawling on my belly in the mud in the middle of the night' for the first time in twenty years.

Contractors plucked three shards of shrapnel off the ground, framed them in a crude wooden frame and shipped the morbid little keepsake off to San Diego with the inscription, 'Dear boss, happy November 1st. ... P.S., we want more money!'

Reichardt began keeping a loaded AR-15 by his cot. 'Not to sound melodramatic,' he wrote, 'but our people are in ever-present danger for their very lives, and I kid you not.'

'To illustrate,' he continued, 'whenever I go to the john, about half a block from our sleeping quarters, all the way there and back I look for the nearest ditch into which to dive on short notice, if necessary.'

Following the raid there was a lull in Lightning Bug missions. Flights resumed on November 7. Eight days later, the Chinese shot down a Model 147B over southern China. Officials in Beijing celebrated the shoot-down as a 'major victory', according to state media.

The *New York Times* reported the story the following day. 'This was the first report from Beijing or elsewhere that pilotless aircraft were being used for reconnaissance,' the *Times* explained.

'The United States is believed to have relied mainly on the Chinese Nationalists for aerial reconnaissance over China to avoid giving Beijing a chance to make propaganda capital out of captured American pilots,' the paper continued. 'The use of pilotless planes would enable the United States to make its own flights without concern over the possibility.'

US officials pretended they had no idea what the Chinese, or the media for that matter, were talking about. 'I know nothing about it,' White House press secretary George Reedy said. 'This is the first I've heard of it.' The State Department said it had no information on the matter. 'No comment,' a Pentagon spokesman muttered.

The denials would become moot seven months later. In April 1965, authorities in Beijing put on display the wreckage of all three Model 147s Chinese forces had by then shot down. Tens of thousands of everyday Chinese shuffled through the Military Museum of the Chinese People's Revolution in Beijing to view the wrecked American robots.

The visitors included Australian-American newspaper reporter Lisa Hobbs, who had traveled to China with an Australian tour group. Hobbs specifically asked the group to swing by the museum so she could see for herself the American drones.

Hobbs described the experience as 'profoundly upsetting'. Observing truckloads of Chinese young people arriving to inspect what museum officials described as 'proof' of American aggression, Hobbs' hands began shaking with patriotic fervor.

In conjunction with the display, the Chinese Communist Party also released a photo of the first drone it shot down the previous November. The image depicted the Lightning Bug shortly after it came down in a field in southern China, crumpled but more or less in one piece.

The press in Japan got its hands on that photo as well as at least one more picture depicting all three shot down Model 147s. In early April 1965 the pictures appeared in US newspapers.

The Air Force's secret was out. Back in November 1964, a photographer who apparently visited Bien Hoa in order to report on Viet Cong attacks on the base had snapped a shot of three Model 147s on dolleys in and around a hangar at the base.

Apparently bowing to pressure from the Pentagon, the photographer's agency, Wide World Photos, initially declined to publish the picture. However, after the

Chinese released their images of the Model 147s, Wide World Photos decided there was no point in withholding its own images.

Now the whole world knew that the Air Force had spy drones in South Vietnam and was sending them into China. The team at OL-20 collectively shrugged. 'This was more or less expected here,' Reichardt wrote to Schwanhausser.

Reichardt suspected that SAC had *wanted* the Chinese to shoot down that first drone. 'Possibly the goal was a deliberate attempt to find out exactly what they [the Chinese] could or could not do,' Reichardt wrote.

Schwanhausser later related to historian Wagner rumors he had heard about the November 1964 shoot-down. As many as twenty Chinese MiGs chased the Lightning Bug as it zoomed over southern China, Schwanhausser reported hearing. The fighters purportedly made between thirty and fifty passes at the drone before finally hitting it.

'We had their attention,' Schwanhausser quipped. 'They were mad.' By late April 1965 the Chinese had shot down five Lightning Bugs. That same month signaled a profound shift in the war over Vietnam. It was in April 1965 that the first of around 2,300 Soviet air-defense troops deployed to North Vietnam to help local forces build up their surface-to-air missile network. S-75s soon followed.

〔左〕撃墜されたアメリカ
の無人偵察機。完全な姿では
ないが、どうやら、ターボジ
ェット推進のＢＱＭ-34Ａファ
イアビーの特殊偵察型のよう
である。1965年5月に中国領
土内で撃墜されて問題になっ
たのも、南ベトナムを基地と
しているＣ-130から発進し た
この特殊偵察型であった。こ
の無人機は超低空をものすご
いスピードで進攻するとい ぅ

In April 1965, authorities in Beijing put on display the wreckage of all three Model 147s Chinese forces had by then shot down. Tens of thousands of everyday Chinese shuffled through the Military Museum of the Chinese People's Revolution in Beijing to view the wrecked American robots. In conjunction with the display, the Chinese Communist Party also released a photo of the first drone it shot down the previous November. The image, reproduced here, depicted the Lightning Bug shortly after it came down in a field in southern China, crumpled but more or less in one piece. (*Teledyne Ryan photo courtesy of the San Diego Air and Space Museum Archive*)

On November 1, 1964 Viet Cong guerrillas closed to within a quarter-mile of Bien Hoa Air Base near Saigon and peppered the flight line with almost 100 81mm mortar shells. The attack destroyed twelve US and South Vietnamese aircraft. Incredibly, no U-2s, Lightning Bugs or DC-130s were even damaged in the raid. No one from the 4080th SRW, military or civilian, was hurt. The attack enraged senior US military leaders, but President Lyndon Johnson, facing an election in just a few days, declined to retaliate. (*US Air Force photo*)

A Viet Cong mortar attack on Bien Hoa Air Base in November 1964 killed four Americans, wounded seventy-two and marked a major escalation in hostilities. This photo depicts US Air Force crews cleaning up the wreckage of destroyed Air Force B-57 bombers in the aftermath of the attack. (*US Air Force photo*)

Through 1964 South Vietnam became increasingly dangerous for US personnel. A Viet Cong truck-bombing targeting the Brinks Hotel in Saigon on Christmas Eve 1964 killed 2 Americans and injured 107 Americans and Vietnamese. (*US Air Force photo*)

# Chapter Nine

In July 1965 the Soviet Union formally agreed to supply S-75 surface-to-air missile systems to North Vietnam. By then a Soviet-led training program for Vietnamese missile crews was already well under way in the Soviet Union as well as at ten camps in North Vietnam.

The first North Vietnamese S-75 regiments actually had Soviet crews. Soviet officers would command Vietnamese S-75 units until the late 1960s. Four Soviet missileers died in combat during the Vietnam War, victims of increasingly deadly US defense-suppression missions.

The Soviet-supplied, Soviet-staffed and Soviet-led North Vietnamese S-75 batteries entered combat on July 24, 1965, when two batteries of the 236th SAM Regiment near Hanoi fired on a flight of US Air Force F-4C fighters, shooting down one jet.

The Air Force hastily organized a retaliatory strike targeting the 236th SAM Regiment. Hoping to exploit the low-altitude gap in the Fan Song radar's coverage, on July 27 the Air Force sent in fifty-four F-105 fighter-bombers.

However, regiment commander Colonel M. Tsygankov anticipated the attack. He dispersed his batteries, replacing them with dummy launchers and surrounding the dummies with 120 anti-aircraft guns.

The F-105s flew into a wall of gunfire. Six F-105s and an RF-101 recce plane tumbled to the ground in flames.

A few weeks later in August 1965 the Navy blundered into a similar ambush, losing five planes during a failed raid on an S-75 regiment.

SAC flew into action, deploying Model 147 drones in an effort to deliberately bait enemy air defenses.

The command pulled out of storage the two Model 147Ds that the Air Force had bought for operations over Cuba back in 1962 and shipped them alongside three new three Model 147Es to Bien Hoa Air Base in South Vietnam, the RB-47s that worked alongside the Long Arm drones deployed to the Philippines.

The Model 147Ds were no-contrail Model 147C airframes with an added sensor for detecting SAM fuze signals. The Model 147Es carried the same sensor but used the Model 147B airframe.

SAC installed a clever bit of technology on both models. A 'traveling wave tube' is a vacuum tube that amplifies radio frequencies. The command designed TWTs that broadcast the same signal that a U-2 returned when irradiated by a Fan Song radar.

Both drone types had one main mission: locate S-75 batteries and capture their signals.

The Model 147Ds went first. They didn't last long. The first mission on August 20, 1965 ended with North Vietnamese forces shooting down the drone with gunfire. No opportunity to bait an S-75 battery.

The second mission on August 31, 1965 also ended with gunners on the ground shooting down the drone. Not that it mattered. The RB-47 suffered an equipment malfunction and couldn't have received data from the Model 147D even if the drone had succeeded in baiting an S-75.

With that, SAC had expended all of its operational Model 147Ds. The Model 147Es went next. Their first sortie took place on October 16, 1965. The drone's sensors and traveling wave tube failed twenty seconds after launch.

It went on to fly a leisurely loop around North Vietnamese air space. No S-75s engaged the unmanned aerial vehicle. 'It wasn't augmented and so didn't look like anything the North Vietnamese wanted to waste a missile on,' Weaver explained. Unmolested, the drone parachuted to a safe recovery.

The second and third missions on October 20 and November 6, 1965 were more successful. Each ended with the drone's destruction, but on both sorties the Model 147Es managed to capture some signals from S-75 batteries, although not the batteries' fuzing signals.

The October mission came away with one incredible image. The Lightning Bug managed to snap a 35mm photo of an incoming V-750 seconds before it exploded.

There was just one Long Arm Model 147E left. Schwanhausser did some troubleshooting on the drone's electronics and determined they were overheating. SAC briefly sent the Model 147E back to the United States for maintenance and upgrade.

On February 13, 1966 the drone flew into North Vietnam, its radar reflector all but announcing its location to the S-75 batteries down below.

At least one V-750 arced into the sky. Finally, the Long Arm drone worked the way SAC and the CIA intended it to. The drone's sensitive radio listening gear scooped up the V-750 fuzing signal and relayed it to a supporting EB-66 electronic warfare plane right before the missile blew the drone out of the sky.

It had taken nearly four years, but US analysts finally had the data they wanted on the V-750's fuze. Eugene Fubini, the assistant secretary of defense for research and engineering, described the February 1966 Long Arm mission as 'the most significant contribution to electronic reconnaissance in the last twenty years'.

The Navy took the data from the Long Arm mission and passed it along to a company called Applied Technology. Three months later the California company installed the first AN/APR-26 radar-warning receivers on Navy fighters flying over North Vietnam.

It was an ingenious system. An array of postcard-size antennas detected the S-75's various signals as well as signals from other air-defense systems. The AN/APR-26 alerted the crew three ways. A cockpit panel flashed warning lights. An alarm-clock-sized, round TV screen flashed little line segments indicating the type of enemy sensor, the sensor's azimuth relative to the targeted plane and the signal strength. Finally, an alarm tone sounded in the cockpit.

The redundant warnings worked. Alerted by the AN/APR-26, crews could take evasive action and dodge incoming V-750s. Or, better still, altogether avoid the S-75's engagement zone. To meet exploding military demand for the radar warning receivers, Applied Technology added 1,200 workers to its 200-strong payroll. Through 1966 and 1967 the company churned out 250 AN/APR-26s every month.

In a poetic twist, the Model 147H recce drone that flew its first combat mission over South-East Asia in March 1967 boasted its own radar warning receiver (RWR). Detecting an approaching V-750, the RWR would trigger an automated maneuver. The Lightning Bug would pull a hard right turn, a maneuver Ryan Aeronautical believed would give the drone its best shot of avoiding the attack.

SAC apparently conducted follow-on SAM-baiting drone missions in late 1966. The details of this mission, code-named 'Old Bar', have never been fully reported, although historian William Cahill found documentation of five operational sorties between October and November 1966 involving 'an unknown variant of the Model 147 drone'.

Photo-reconnaissance Lightning Bug missions continued in parallel with the counter-SAM flights, and in July 1965, OL-20 got a new and more powerful drone, the Model 147G. The G-model Lightning Bug, which was 2ft longer than the B-model, boasted the new T-41A version of the J69 engine with 1,920lb of thrust, 220lb more than the T-29 on the B.

The bigger motor boosted the Lightning Bug's ceiling. Flying higher tended to produce telltale contrails, so Ryan Aeronautical added to the Model 147G the same contrail-suppressing system it had developed for the C-model drone.

There was a downside. All the new equipment added weight and reduced the Model 147G's range compared to the Model 147B.

The Model 147B flew its final mission in December 1965. The Air Force launched seventy-eight sorties with thirty-two operational B-model Lightning Bugs. The drone returned on 62 percent of missions.

Sixty-six Model 147Bs got shot at on their missions. North Vietnamese and Chinese gunners and missileers shot down twelve of them. On average, a Model 147B completed 2.6 missions before crashing or getting blown out of the sky. The longest-lived Model 147B completed eight sorties.

Wagner charitably described the B-model Lightning Bug's performance as 'satisfactory but not spectacular', but by the time the Model 147B was ending its front-line career, the Lightning Bug was finally becoming indispensable.

This was not because the drones were reliable, but because the Air Force could not afford to lose them. The S-75's arrival in North Vietnam and Hanoi's acquisition of MiG-17 fighters was making North Vietnam a deadly place for American pilots. Even the RF-101s, speeding along at low level, were getting swatted from the sky.

After a V-750 nearly struck a U-2 flying over Haiphong Harbor, SAC organized a test. OL-20 launched a Model 147B straight into Hanoi's thickest air defenses, while one of Bien Hoa's U-2s monitored the flight from a distance.

An S-75 battery opened fire. The U-2 pilot watched in horror as the 'telephone pole' missile 'consumed' the drone, Schwanhausser recalled. Over drinks at the Bien Hoa Officers' Club, the U-2 pilot ended the rivalry between the detachment's manned and unmanned recce camps. 'From now on, you guys can have that mission,' the pilot said.

Sure, the Lightning Bug was still an unreliable system, but it was winning the Air Force's favor by default.

The new Model 147Gs promised better performance, but the climate literally rained on the type's parade. The G-models arrived at Bien Hoa just in time for the monsoon season. The drones could fly over the bad weather, but what did that matter when their cameras couldn't see through the clouds?

'We needed to get under the weather,' Weaver explained. As a bonus, SAC believed that low flights might thwart the S-75 batteries.

A colonel at SAC headquarters came up with an idea. He asked Ryan Aeronautical to install the company's new barometric low-altitude control system, plus a low-altitude camera, in some old C-model Lightning Bugs that SAC had stored in Arizona.

The barometric low-altitude control system, or BLACS, was simple in concept. It steadily read the air pressure and, based on that reading, guessed at the drone's altitude and ordered the control surfaces to make adjustments in order to maintain a constant height. Ryan Aeronautical set the BLACS in the Model 147C to 1,500ft, which SAC hoped would be low enough to get underneath monsoon clouds as well as beneath the ballistic arc of a V-750 missile.

The Air Force modified just three Model 147Cs and sent them to OL-20 in early October 1965. They didn't last long. All three disappeared within a couple of weeks.

The Model 147C's final front-line mission on October 12 was a memorable one. The DC-130 flew at just 500ft toward the release point then climbed to 5,000ft to launch the drone. A US electronic-surveillance plane warned the DC-130 crew that an S-75 battery tracked them the whole way.

The first launch attempt ended in an abort owing to a technical malfunction. The DC-130 spent twenty-three minutes flying circles over a bunch of North Vietnamese fishing boats, their occupants angrily shaking their fists at the Americans, while the drone launch crew sorted out the problem. The S-75 was locked on the entire time.

The Lightning Bug finally launched, and then went crazy as the BLACS kicked in. The drone suddenly zoomed to 8,000ft then dove down to 3,000ft before finally settling in at its prescribed 1,500ft cruising altitude.

The DC-130 crew turned south. The Lightning Bug they had risked so much to launch flew into the clouds … and never returned.

The Model 147Gs began flying once the weather cleared up. In just under two years, the 4080th SRW detachment would launch Model 147Gs eighty-three times. The drones returned from just forty-five of the missions.

One mission almost got two members of the 4080th SRW killed. A Model 147G disappeared in bad weather somewhere over Laos. 'Some time later,' according to Wagner, 'a Laotian man found the drone's wreck on a forested hilltop.'

The 4080th SRW dispatched an airman and a Ryan Aeronautical employee to recover the drone. They joined up with some Laotian fighters and flew to the crash site in a helicopter belonging to Air America, the CIA's covert air wing in Laos.

They were just beginning to inspect the drone when one of the Laotians triggered a mortar-bomb booby-trap. The mortar hissed. Everyone ran. The booby-trap was faulty and didn't explode, but the distant sound of drums signaled an approaching enemy force.

The recovery team fled. US forces later bombed the crash site.

A US Air Force RF-101C manned recce plane photographed its own shadow during a low-altitude pass over a damaged bridge in North Vietnam. With North Vietnamese air defenses growing denser and more sophisticated through 1965, the speedy RF-101s began suffering such a high attrition rate that the Air Force soon had little choice but to ramp up drone operations. (*US Air Force photo*)

The single-seat RF-101C was the US Air Force's primary *manned* day-reconnaissance aircraft for much of the Vietnam War. A variant of a mostly unsuccessful interceptor and fighter-bomber, the RF-101 excelled in the recce role owing to its high supersonic speed, but it suffered a relatively high loss rate in the course of around 35,000 missions. Of the 166 RF-101Cs that the Air Force acquired, 33 crashed during an operational sortie or were destroyed in combat. Surface-to-air missiles and anti-aircraft guns accounted for most of the shoot-downs. A North Vietnamese MiG-21 in September 1967 shot down one RF-101C. (*US Air Force photo*)

The Long Arm drone missions that collected V-750 fuzing data in 1965 and '66 led to the development of the AN/APR-26 radar-warning receiver. The system's array of small antennas detected the S-75's various signals as well as signals from other air-defense systems and alerted the crew with flashing lights and other visual cues as well as an alarm tone. Applied Technology in California churned out more than 200 AN/APR-26s every month through the late 1960s, possibly saving the lives of hundreds of air crew. The white object on the upper right side of this F-4C cockpit, on display at the National Museum of the United States Air Force, is the AN/APR-26 display. (*US Air Force photo*)

# Chapter Ten

The Model 147G's 54 percent return rate was significantly worse than the Model 147B's 62 percent return rate. Strategic Air Command in part blamed the December 1965 pause in the American bombing campaign.

On December 17, 1965, President Lyndon Johnson met with his advisors in the White House. Johnson wanted to halt the air campaign over South-East Asia in order to give diplomats a chance to work out some kind of peace agreement that might end the war.

Secretary of Defense McNamara warned Johnson that the Joint Chiefs of Staff would oppose de-escalation. Johnson was insistent. 'Try to sell our enemies that we want peace,' he said. 'We owe this to the American people. We can't do this if we are dropping bombs on the enemy.'

The bombing pause began on December 24, 1965 and lasted until January 30, 1966. The military halted raids by manned aircraft but continued to send reconnaissance aircraft, including Lightning Bugs, north into enemy territory.

The drones flew into a solid wall of enemy fire. Twenty-four missions resulted in the loss of sixteen Model 147s, ten of them new G-models. 'Without the confusion of an accompanying air strike, the unmanned Ryan birds became very vulnerable north of the demilitarized zone and so the attrition rate went up sharply,' Wagner explained.

SAC in a panic pleaded with Ryan Aeronautical to develop a decoy drone to fly along with the camera-equipped Lightning Bugs in order to draw away missiles and gunfire. Ryan Aeronautical said it could do it, no problem. The requirement was so urgent that the Air Force waived all normal acquisitions rules.

Ryan Aeronautical employee Dale Weaver paired up with Major Harold Smith, an Air Force maintenance officer at Davis-Monthan Air Force Base in Arizona, where much of the Lightning Bug development took place.

For two weeks in early 1966 Weaver and Smith scoured Air Force depots for equipment. They located ten early-model Lightning Bugs and, enlisting airmen for 'free' labor, over a period of ten days installed on the drones traveling wave tubes that boosted their radar signatures.

These Model 147N decoys arrived at Bien Hoa in March 1966. 'The theory was to launch one of the high-altitude G or other operational birds almost simultaneously with an N decoy,' Reichardt explained. 'They would be programmed to fly parallel for a while and then diverge as they approached the target area,' he added. 'The split pattern would confuse the enemy's ground radars by giving them a choice of two birds at which to fire.'

The Lightning Bug team didn't expect the Model 147Ns to return from their missions. There were no plans to recover them, so Ryan Aeronautical replaced the drones' parachutes with sandbags. This resulted in a few farces on those rare missions where the decoy drones managed to avoid enemy fire. The decoys returned to Da Nang and circled until their fuel ran out.

However, on most missions, the Model 147Ns did what Ryan Aeronautical designed them to do. They flew high, broadcasting a huge radar signature and drew fire from North Vietnamese air-defenders.

The Model 147Ns also managed to 'shoot down' five North Vietnamese fighters, albeit indirectly, when the fighters ran out of fuel chasing the decoys. A North Vietnamese SAM battery accidentally shot down one MiG that was in hot pursuit of a drone. A MiG in similar fashion inadvertently shot down a second MiG that was tailing a Model 147N.

The 4080th SRW expended all the Model 147Ns in the course of nine missions between March and June 1966. Strategic Air Command in August 1966 placed an order for ten more decoys. The command hoped the new decoys might draw fire from its lumbering B-52s.

Ryan Aeronautical modified another batch of older Model 147s into Model 174NXs, this time adding a recovery parachute plus a simple camera with 6ft resolution. The camera on the recce Model 147s shot at a resolution of 1ft. That way, if a decoy did manage to survive its mission, it could also feed some film to the processing lab in Saigon. Who knew what kind of intelligence the Air Force might derive from it? 'Trucks and things like that could be identified,' Wagner noted.

SAC headquarters wanted more low-altitude drones, but Schwanhausser pushed back. 'I didn't think it was a very good idea,' he explained, citing the Model 147C's abortive career, but SAC insisted. The command gave Ryan Aeronautical one day to draw up a proposal and one month to produce the first airframe.

Ryan Aeronautical decided to base the new, low-flying drone on the high-altitude Model 147G it was already producing. The first Model 147J was ready for testing in January 1966.

Aerodynamically, the J was a dog. Its big wing, a feature the J-model inherited from the G-model on which it was based, was more efficient at altitude.

One test flight over California on January 3, 1966 nearly ended in disaster when the drone sharply pitched up shortly after launch and collided with the DC-130 mothership. The collision demolished the drone and knocked the propellers off the DC-130's number four engine.

The first three J-models all suffered catastrophic failures during trials. The fourth J worked as designed, however. It flew seven successful test flights before Ryan Aeronautical shipped it to Bien Hoa for operational missions.

Model 147J-4 flew five good missions in three months starting in March 1966.

In ramping up low-level flights with the Lightning Bugs, the team at Bien Hoa discovered a flaw in the drone's systems, one that wasn't evident or even problematic on high-level flights. Many of the low-level Lightning Bugs launched perfectly, successfully avoided getting shot up and even recovered without incident, but their missions were still failures.

This was because, it turned out, they flew a course that was just a few miles to the left or right of a track that would bring them over the target. At high altitude, a few miles didn't make any difference to a camera whose side-to-side field of view might be 100 miles or more.

However, at low altitude, the camera might see just a mile across. If the drone's flight path deviated by a few miles, it might result in the vehicle photographing … nothing of interest. Trees. Villages. Rice paddies.

The problem actually started with the C-130 launch plane. The mothership's Doppler radar was accurate only to a few miles, meaning it was entirely possible the C-130 would be a few miles off-course when it launched its Lightning Bugs.

Meanwhile the drones' own navigation systems were accurate only to around 3 percent of the distance the aircraft traveled from the launch point. After a few hundred miles, a Lightning Bug might be as far as 12 miles off course. In that case, its film probably captured nothing useful.

Fewer than half of the low-level missions succeeded in capturing imagery of their intended targets.

The navigation inaccuracy was a fixture of the J-model low-level drones, but the J-models also helped to introduce major advancements in drone operations.

The Model 147J boasted two cameras instead of the one on earlier Lightning Bugs. Where older drones had just the front-to-back scanning camera, the J also featured a side-to-side camera.

The arrangement resulted in some remarkable photographs. On one mission, Model 147J-14 snapped a photo of a North Vietnamese surface-to-air missile barely missing the drone. The J's low-level photos of ships in Haiphong Harbor were 'unbelievable', according to one Ryan Aeronautical employee.

The J's excellent photography was no accident. It was the first Lightning Bug to carry two cameras: the standard, downward-looking Hycon HR233 camera with its

24in focal length, plus a Fairchild KA-60 for side-to-side scans that captured the ground beneath the drone from horizon to horizon.

The KA-60, like all contemporary panoramic cameras, was an engineering marvel. It managed to produce reasonably high-resolution, wide-angle photos with a lens that wasn't wide. To accomplish this, Fairchild added a cylindrical prism in front of the lens. The prism rotated, compensating for the drone's forward movement as the camera peered from side to side.

Granted, with its 3in focal length and 4.5in by 9.4in format, the KA-60 was a lower-fidelity camera than the Hycon Model 233, but in photographing from horizon to horizon, it mitigated the navigational drift that plagued all low-level Lightning Bug missions.

Another advancement that coincided with the Model 147J's arrival in South Vietnam resulted in a profound overall improvement in the Lightning Bugs' usefulness.

On four of the initial Model 147J missions in the spring of 1966, the Air Force recovered the drone by way of its new 'mid-air retrieval system', or MARS.

MARS entailed a cargo plane or helicopter trailing a long hook to snag a payload while it was descending toward Earth under a parachute. The Air Force first deployed MARS on the C-119 cargo plane during tests of early Q-2 target drones in 1955.

Starting in 1959, the National Reconnaissance Office borrowed the method, equipping C-119s and C-130s to snatch film capsules from the earliest Corona spy satellites. The US Army tinkered with a similar concept, but using helicopters instead of cargo planes.

However, by 1965 the Army program was idle for a lack of funding. A Ryan Aeronautical employee named Fred Yochim heard a rumor about the Army effort and tracked down the captain who had flown the test recoveries for the ground-combat branch at a base in New Mexico.

The captain happily handed over his records and equipment. Yochim showed it to the Air Force. 'We got the program up and going,' Yochim recalled.

Modified for helicopters and drones, MARS worked like this. The drone deployed its recovery parachute at 15,000ft over the recovery zone. The main 'chute trailed a smaller 'chute. For the MARS crew, the latter was the target.

Flying 3,000ft below the drone as it popped its main 'chute, the helicopter crew angled toward the secondary 'chute, aiming to snag that 'chute's line with the grappling hook extending aft from the 'copter's belly.

After the helicopter grabbed the line, a mechanism on the main 'chute collapsed the larger canopy. Now the drone was hanging more or less free from the helicopter.

The 'copter crew reeled in the drone until it trailed just 15ft or so from the rotorcraft. The crew then flew the drone back to base and gently deposited it on the tarmac.

MARS radically improved the Lightning Bug program's mission success rate. Whereas before there was a roughly even chance of a recovery failing or at least damaging the film – to say nothing of endangering the soldiers whose job it was to retrieve landed drones – with MARS, missions that didn't result in a shoot-down or a crash almost always ended in a successful recovery.

Between 1966 and the end of the Vietnam War, Army helicopters attempted 2,745 mid-air drone recoveries and completed 2,655 of them; a 96.7 percent success rate.

The US Air Force developed the 'mid-air retrieval system' or MARS in the 1950s. MARS entailed a cargo plane or helicopter trailing a long hook to snag a payload while it was descending toward Earth under a parachute. The Air Force first deployed MARS on the C-119 cargo plane during tests of early Q-2 target drones in 1955. The US Army tinkered with a similar concept, but using helicopters instead of cargo planes. By 1965, failed parachute-recoveries posed a major problem for the Model 147 drone program. A Ryan Aeronautical employee heard a rumor about the Army effort and tracked down the captain who had flown the test recoveries at a base in New Mexico. Within a year, the Lightening Bug detachment in Vietnam was flying CH-3 helicopters to conduct MARS recoveries, significantly boosting the rate of successful recoveries for the Model 147 force. (*US Air Force art*)

The US Air Force, Army and Navy used a variety of helicopters to retrieve target drones following the drones' parachute-recovery. Any helicopter with a winch and adequate lifting power would do, such as the Army's CH-37 pictured here. However, when the Air Force introduced mid-air drone recovery in 1966, the service also settled on the new, more powerful CH-3 helicopter as the primary recovery platform. (*Teledyne Ryan photo courtesy of the San Diego Air and Space Museum Archive*)

The Sikorsky CH-3 helicopter became US Strategic Air Command's standard helicopter for drone-support missions. The CH-3s transported recovery crews, lifted drones back to base from their rural landing zones and, following the 1966 introduction of the Mid-Air Recovery System, snatched Lightning Bugs from the air as they descended underneath their parachutes at the end of their sorties. (*Teledyne Ryan photo courtesy of the San Diego Air and Space Museum Archive*)

The Mid-Air Retrieval System hugely boosted the Lightning Bug's recovery rate. Flying 3,000ft below the drone as it popped its main 'chute, a CH-3 helicopter crew angled toward the secondary 'chute, aiming to snag that 'chute's line with the grappling hook extending aft from the 'copter's belly. After the helicopter grabbed the line, a mechanism on the main 'chute collapsed the larger canopy. Now the drone was hanging more or less free from the helicopter. The 'copter crew reeled in the drone until it trailed just 15ft or so from the rotorcraft. The crew then flew the drone back to base and gently deposited it on the tarmac. (*Teledyne Ryan photo courtesy of the San Diego Air and Space Museum Archive*)

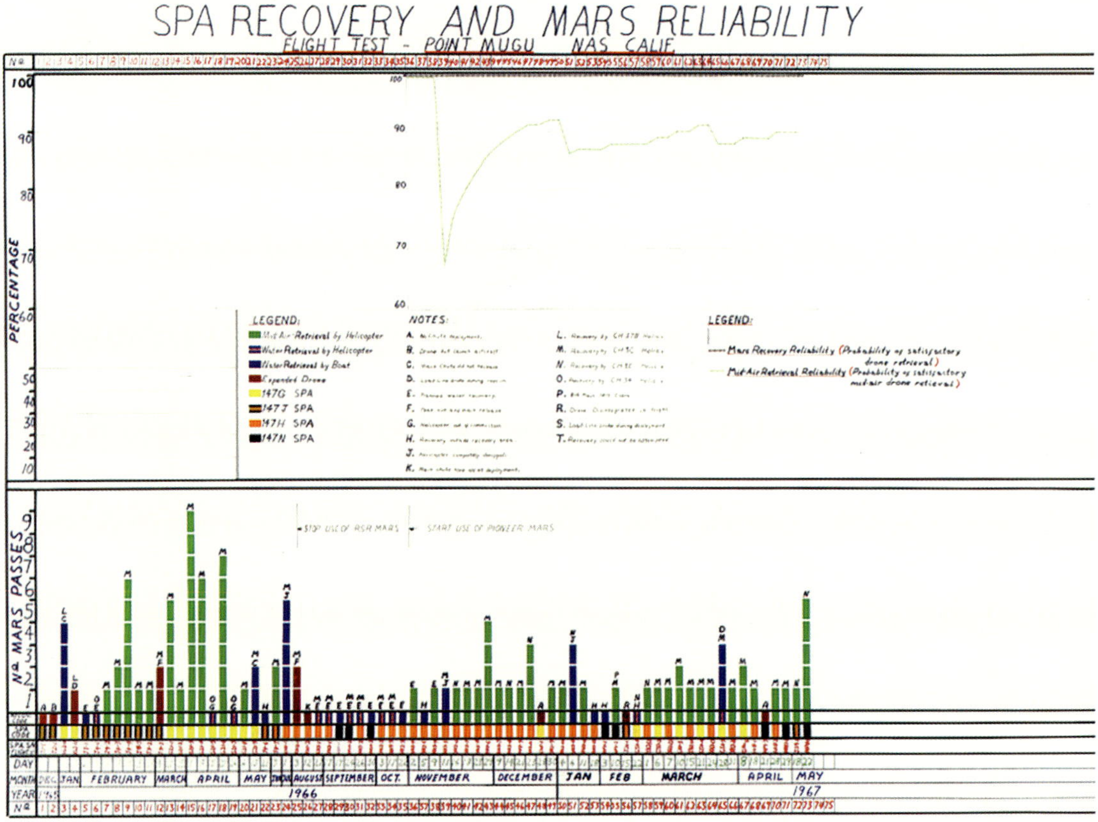

The introduction of the Mid-Air Retrieval System in 1966 greatly improved the recovery rate for Model 147 drones. MARS entailed a helicopter trailing a long hook to snag a drone while it was descending toward Earth under a parachute. The improvement in recovery rates was evident even in the Model 147 test effort in the United States, as this hand-drawn chart testifies. The green line at the top illustrates a big boost in successful recoveries as MARS became routine. (*Teledyne Ryan photo courtesy of the San Diego Air and Space Museum Archive*)

## Chapter Eleven

The low-flying Model 147Js between March 1966 and November 1967 flew ninety-four front-line missions, returning 65 percent of the time.

The J-models' missions largely overlapped with those of the G-models, helping to boost the number of operational drone launches from 77 in 1965 to 105 in '66. An important one-off model took flight in July 1966.

At the same time that Applied Technology was designing the AN/APR-26 based on signals the Model 147E had acquired, engineers working for the Navy were developing a jammer that could disrupt the S-75's main Fan Song radar.

The AN/ALQ-51 jammer was ready in mid-1966. Ryan Aeronautical took a single Model 147B Lightning Bug, hung the Navy's pod on it, redesignated it 'Model 147F' and flew it over North Vietnam with jammers blaring.

The idea was simple. The AN/ALQ-51 received the signal from the S-75's Fan Song radar, held onto it for a brief interval then rebroadcast it back to the S-75 battery. The delay could help convince the S-75 operators that the target aircraft was at a different location than it actually was.

On that first test mission, the AN/ALQ-51 worked. It took ten V-750s to shoot down the Model 147F. Secretary of Defense Robert McNamara himself tracked the F-model's flight and was pleased. 'We had a bird that had the capability to go and test equipment in the real live environment without risking a man's life,' Schwanhausser explained.

Flight ops from OL-20 further expanded in 1967. That spring, the Lightning Bug team was simultaneously operating three different drone types: the G, the J and the NX decoy. H-models arrived in February 1967 and began flying missions in the following month.

The Model 147H represented a major effort by the Air Force and Ryan Aeronautical to advance the state of the art in drone technology. It, like the Model 147G, was a high-flier, cruising at 65,000ft. That high ceiling demanded changes to the airframe as well as to the J69 T-41A engine. Ryan Aeronautical removed from the Model 147H the heavy contrail-suppressing system that was standard on older, high-altitude drone models.

To boost the H's range to 2,400 miles, Ryan Aeronautical redesigned the model's wing, adding integral fuel tanks. The company also piled new defensive aids into the

Model 147H, including a radar-absorbing coating in the inlet duct plus a jammer that went by the code-name of 'Rivet Bounder' as well as 'Hat Rack', a system that prompted evasive maneuvers.

Rivet Bounder was similar in concept to the ALQ-51. When a Fan Song guidance signal touched the system's antenna, Rivet Bounder responded by transmitting via the same antenna a modified drone radar signature that, on the enemy's scope, placed the aircraft in a different location than it really was. At least, that's what it did in theory.

When a V-750 was incoming, Hat Rack would detect the missile's own radar pulses and initiate a high-energy maneuver by the drone that, its designers hoped, would help it to dodge the missile. Another mode on Hat Rack detected a MiG fighter's radar signal and prompted the drone to conduct a 90-degree evasive turn.

In design, the defensive systems were ambitious, perhaps overly so. 'Neither Rivet Bounder nor Hat Rack was more than partially successful,' one Air Force historian concluded.

In early 1967 the high-altitude Model 147Hs flew in parallel with the low-altitude Model 147Js. However, the Js for all their success still had a one-in-three chance of crashing or getting shot down on any given mission.

SAC crunched the numbers and projected it would run out of Js before the next low-flying Lightning Bug, the Model 147S, was ready in late 1967. So the command cut a check and told Ryan Aeronautical to produce an interim low-flyer, and do it fast.

Just like it had one with the Model 147N decoy, Ryan Aeronautical searched Air Force warehouses for old Model 147As with J69-T-29A motors. The company packed into the old As the same two-camera set-up that it had devised for the Model 147J.

The result was the Model 147NP. It was underpowered compared to the J, but it was better than nothing. It also was the basis for the first version of the Lightning Bug specifically fitted out for night-time operations.

In response to US air strikes, the Viet Cong had increasingly shifted to nocturnal operations. Troops and supply convoys moved along jungle trails under the cover of darkness. The Air Force was desperate to pinpoint these trails.

SAC told Ryan Aeronautical to pull four Model 147NPs from the production line. Under the supervision of Ed Christian, a former Marine Corps recce expert, the company installed a white-light strobe in the drones and synchronized it with the cameras.

It wasn't a perfect system. Sure, the Model 147NRE night-recce drone might be able to take photos in the dark, but a blinding flash of light accompanied every frame. It gave itself away at a rate of one flash per second.

Unsurprisingly, the four Model 147NREs had the worst return rate of any Lightning Bug variant. They flew just seven missions starting in May 1967, returning on average 43 percent of the time. OL-20 launched its last Model 147NRE mission in September 1967.

However, a sortie on June 5, 1967 was the NRE's most memorable. The drone's main recovery parachute separated, plunging the vehicle into the jungle north of Da Nang.

Christian volunteered to help recover the drone. He grabbed a pistol and an M16 and boarded an SAC CH-3 helicopter along with a Marine Corps explosive-ordnance disposal (EOD) team. The EOD team was insurance. If Christian couldn't bring back the Lightning Bug, the Marines would blow it up.

As they angled toward the crash site, the Americans realized they had competition. A Viet Cong patrol was working its way through the trees toward the crash site. The helicopter crew winched Christian into a patch of elephant grass that quickly sliced up his exposed skin. He was a bloody mess by the time he hacked his way to the Lightning Bug.

'It wasn't in too bad shape,' Christian later told Wagner. He removed the film canisters and sent them up to the hovering CH-3. Low on fuel, the helicopter sped away. Two Marine Corps gunships showed up to cover Christian, but the contractor worried that the helicopters might also lead the Viet Cong straight to his position.

Christian assumed it would be impossible to recover the Lightning Bug. He hacked a hole in the drone's fuel tank and shot up the camera suite with his borrowed M16. That's when a back-up CH-3 arrived, dangling a hook for the Model 147 that Christian was busy trying to destroy.

As the helicopter pulled up and away, 40 gallons of fuel spilled from the drone's punctured tank and dowsed Christian. He was bloody and covered in highly-flammable drone gas when the first CH-3 reappeared to pluck him from the jungle. The gunships opened fire on the nearby Viet Cong to cover the retreat.

The weather was particularly nasty over Vietnam in the fall of 1967, putting a damper on Lightning Bug operations. Weaver even blamed the loss of Model 147H-14 on a thunderstorm that he said might have interfered with the drone's electrical system. 'We'll give 'em Hell if the weather will just clear for a while,' Weaver wrote.

In late 1967 and into '68, it was the North Vietnamese, the Chinese and even the US Navy that gave the Lightning Bug team Hell, not the other way around. The shoot-downs coincided with the Tet Offensive, a coordinated assault by North Vietnamese forces targeting 100 cities and outposts in South Vietnam between January and September 1968.

This circa 1967 photo depicts the 100th Strategic Reconnaissance Wing's drone detachment at Bien Hoa Air Base in South Vietnam. Four Model 147s are visible, as is the detachment's DC-130. On the opposite side of the protective wall, fuel bladders are visible, and beside them, US Air Force F-100 fighter-bombers. Bien Hoa was the target of several damaging Viet Cong raids. As the tide of war turned against the United States and South Vietnam in mid-1970, the 100th SRW moved to U Tapao Air Base in southern Thailand. (*Teledyne Ryan photo courtesy of the San Diego Air and Space Museum Archive*)

In early 1967 the high-altitude Model 147Hs flew in parallel with the low-altitude Model 147Js. Yet the Js, for all their success, still had a one in three chance of crashing or getting shot down on any given mission. (*Teledyne Ryan photo courtesy of the San Diego Air and Space Museum Archive*)

To boost the Model 147H's range to 2,400 miles, Ryan Aeronautical redesigned the drone's wing, adding integral fuel tanks. The company also piled new defensive aids into the Model 147H, including a radar-absorbing coating in the inlet duct plus a jammer that went by the code-name 'Rivet Bounder' as well as 'Hat Rack', a system that prompted evasive maneuvers. (*Teledyne Ryan photo courtesy of the San Diego Air and Space Museum Archive*)

The Model 147H represented a major effort by the US Air Force and Ryan Aeronautical to advance the state of the art in drone technology. It, like the Model 147G, was a high-flier, cruising at 65,000ft. That high ceiling demanded changes to the airframe as well as to the J69 T-41A engine. Ryan Aeronautical removed from the Model 147H the heavy contrail-suppressing system that was standard on older, high-altitude drone models. (*Teledyne Ryan photo courtesy of the San Diego Air and Space Museum Archive*)

Ryan Aeronautical from the beginning of the Lightning Bug program worked hard to reduce the drone's radar signature. Early efforts included stapling sheets of radar-absorbing material to the drones' fuselage. These measures lost effectiveness as enemy air defenses improved, so Ryan Aeronautical developed new stealth features for the Model 147H, which flew its first front-line missions in March 1967. To make the Model 147H appear smaller on enemy radar screens, Ryan Aeronautical applied an RAM coating in the type's jet intake, which with its sharp angles was a major source of radar reflectivity. (*Teledyne Ryan photo courtesy of the San Diego Air and Space Museum Archive*)

The Rivet Bounder system was supposed to help the Model 147H dodge enemy S-75 batteries. When a Fan Song guidance signal touched the system's antenna, Rivet Bounder responded by transmitting via the same antenna a modified drone radar signature that, on the enemy's scope, placed the aircraft in a different location to where it really was. This photo depicts a Model 147H during testing. Frontline Model 147Hs sported a black paint scheme. (*Teledyne Ryan photo courtesy of the San Diego Air and Space Museum Archive*)

In February 1967 OL-20 at Bien Hoa in South Vietnam operated four versions of the Model 147 Lightning Bug drone. Clockwise from top, the Model 147H was a long-range, high-altitude recce drone. The Model 147G was a basic medium-altitude B-model Lightning Bug but with a more powerful engine. The Model 147NX was a low-altitude decoy. The Model 147J was the first purpose-built low-altitude recce drone. (*Teledyne Ryan photo courtesy of the San Diego Air and Space Museum Archive*)

# MODEL 147 NRE (4)

In 1967, Ryan Aeronautical had modified a few Model 147As to produce Model 147NREs for nighttime operations. In a similar fashion, the company pulled twenty Model 147Ss off the San Diego production line and modified them for night ops, complete with a sinister black paint scheme. Whereas the NRE had a white-light strobe that gave away its position with every flash, the Model 147SRE had an infrared strobe, making it all but invisible to enemy troops on the ground. (*Teledyne Ryan photo courtesy of the San Diego Air and Space Museum Archive*)

A Model 147S drone flying at low level snapped this photo of North Vietnamese anti-aircraft gun positions in October 1968. The inset photo on the right is from the drone's smaller panoramic camera. The addition of a panoramic camera in Ryan Aeronautical drones starting in early 1966 greatly improved the quality of the imagery they collected. Panoramic cameras featured a cylindrical prism in front of the lens. The prism rotated, compensating for the drone's forward movement as the camera peered from side to side. (*US Air Force photo*)

# Chapter Twelve

Chinese forces by April '68 had shot down eighteen Model 147s, including four H-models in quick succession in January and March that year. North Vietnamese gunners in late April shot down Model 147S-39 over Haiphong Harbor.

Adding insult to injury, in May '68 a US Navy fighter pilot patrolling over the Gulf of Tonkin mistook an off-course Model 147 for a North Vietnamese MiG-21 and shot it down. Years later, Ryan Aeronautical awarded the pilot a plaque commemorating his aerial victory.

The Lightning Bug operation clearly had more problems than just the weather. It was becoming increasingly apparent that North Vietnamese forces had advance knowledge of the drones' mission starts and flight paths.

When staffers briefed Army General Earle Wheeler, then chairman of the Joint Chiefs of Staff, on their suspicion, Wheeler slammed his fist on the table. 'God damn it,' he roared, 'we've been penetrated!'

Wheeler authorized Operation Purple Dragon, which brought together experts from the National Security Agency, the Defense Intelligence Agency and other military intelligence units. Their mission was to identify the leak and then plug it.

Purple Dragon operatives traveled to South Vietnam to inspect US military communications systems. They concluded that North Vietnamese code-breakers had decrypted US radio signals. The Purple Dragons began installing new encryption across the American force, including at OL-20. The unit's DC-130s got their very first encrypted radios.

'To the surprise of no one on the Purple Dragon team, the very next day the drone loss rate plummeted and stayed down for quite a while,' the NSA stated in an official history. 'Drone losses to enemy action fell off to one or two a year, compared to two or three a week in the pre-Purple Dragon days.'

While the NSA was trying to plug its leak, a greater crisis developed. On April 18, 1969, North Korean MiG-21 fighters shot down a US Navy EC-121 spy plane flying 90 miles off the North Korean coast. All thirty-one Americans aboard the lumbering four-engine plane died.

The Japan-based EC-121 was an electronic-intelligence (ELINT) aircraft. It used its sensitive receivers to register North Korean radars on behalf of the NSA and other agencies.

The Pentagon had shifted the NSA ELINT mission to the Navy's EC-121s after an incident in January 1968 when North Korean forces attacked and captured the Navy ELINT vessel *Pueblo* sailing in international waters off the North Korean coast. One *Pueblo* sailor died in the attack. North Korea held the eighty-two survivors until December '68.

The EC-121 escalated tensions on the Korean Peninsula just fifteen years after the end of the Korean War. President Nixon couldn't afford two wars in East Asia, so he declined to retaliate for the shoot-down. Nor could he afford another shoot-down. Nixon suspended the EC-121 missions.

However, the demand for intelligence on North Korea was, if anything, growing. The Pentagon needed to replace the EC-121s, and fast. Air Force Lieutenant Colonel Andy Corra, upon reading about the spy plane's destruction, promptly got on the phone to Ryan Aeronautical.

The company proposed to modify the Model 147T, a variant of the Model 147H with a more powerful engine, to carry the same kind of ELINT receivers that the much larger EC-121 carried. The Model 147TE would also have a real-time data-link that would allow it to beam raw data straight to a ground station.

The idea was for the Model 147TEs to fly along the periphery of North Korea, feeding intelligence on North Korean forces straight to the NSA. If the North Koreans shot down a few, so what? The Pentagon by 1968 had plenty of experience in shrugging off high-profile Lightning Bug losses.

The military gave the Model 147TEs' mission the code-name 'Combat Dawn'. The Model 147TEs flew from OL-16 at Osan Air Base in South Korea for three years starting in January 1970. In all, OL-16 launched 268 Combat Dawn missions for a 91 percent return rate.

Back in South Vietnam, the introduction of new encryption in mid-1967 dovetailed with the debut of the most important and most successful Lightning Bug model, the Model 147S. It represented Ryan Aeronautical's effort to improve upon the Model 147J for the dangerous low-altitude recce mission.

Various subvariants of the Model 147S flew more than half of all Lightning Bug sorties between December 1967 and the end of the war in 1972. The four longest-serving Lightning Bugs were Model 147SCs, most notably 'Tom Cat', which completed sixty-eight missions compared to just three missions for the typical Lightning Bug.

Walt Raynor, then head of the Pentagon's Big Safari office, kicked off the Model 147S's development with a few pointed hints during a dinner with Ryan Aeronautical's Bob Reichardt in Washington, D.C. some time in late 1966.

'If you guys could come in here with a plan for a low-altitude photo-reconnaissance bird to replace the J at a very low price, just as low as you can get it, I can assure you hundreds will be required,' Raynor said. He mentioned $150,000 per copy as a target price.

In fact, a Model 147S ended up costing $160,000, which was impressively close to Raynor's target.

'The name of the game was to get the price down,' Reichardt recalled. For the Model 147S, Ryan Aeronautical kept the J's 1,920lb-thrust engine but reverted to a smaller, simpler and stiffer wing that had less than half the area than the wing on the J model.

The S was a better low-level performer than the J model. Its smaller wing was stiffer and allowed for a smoother ride. In place of the finicky barometric low-altitude control system, the Model 147S had the new 'multiple altitude control system' (MACS).

MACS had three settings, allowing a Model 147S to climb as high as 20,000ft and dive as low as 1,000ft during a mission. Frequent altitude changes helped the drone to zoom *over* anti-aircraft gunfire and *under* surface-to-air missiles.

The S also swapped out the J's two-camera set-up for a single panoramic camera that returned some truly remarkable images. A Model 147S snapped a series of photos of a V-750 missile flying alongside the drone right before exploding. Incredibly, the drone survived the close encounter with its biggest killer.

On another mission in October 1968, a Model 147S malfunctioned. The drone cruised over North Vietnam at an altitude of just 150ft, so low that it passed under high-tension power lines. The wide panoramic photos from that mission showed, in crisp detail, Vietnamese workers staring in awe at the passing American drone.

The Air Force ordered the S in batches, each with small improvements over the previous batch. The first batch of forty Model 147SAs entered combat in December 1967. They flew ninety missions for a 63 percent return rate. Forty Model 147SBs quickly followed and flew 159 missions, returning 76 percent of the time.

Back in 1967, Ryan Aeronautical had modified a few Model 147As to produce Model 147NREs for night-time operations. In a similar fashion, the company pulled twenty Model 147Ss off the San Diego production line and modified them for night ops, complete with a sinister black paint scheme.

Where the NRE had a white-light strobe that gave away its position with every flash, the Model 147SRE had an infrared strobe, making it all but invisible to enemy troops on the ground. 'You didn't attract anyone's attention unless they were looking directly at it and then the only thing you would actually see was just a red light,' Christian recalled.

The SREs flew forty-four missions between November 1968 and October 1969, returning 73 percent of the time. 'We turned up some interesting things in the way of intelligence,' Weaver said. 'We found that there was a lot more activity at night than the Air Force thought possible.'

On December 19, 1968 Model 147SRE-2 duplicated the missile-photography feat from October '68, snapping a photo of a V-750 missile that barely missed the drone. 'The SAM passed close enough to the camera window that it completely burned out that frame of imagery,' Christian said.

This was the same year that Tactical Air Command, the headquarters that oversaw the Air Force's shorter-range fighters, grew jealous of Strategic Air Command's drones. TAC wanted drones of its own, but not for reconnaissance.

Instead, the command hoped to fly Model 147s on electronic-countermeasures missions in order to protect TAC fighters from North Vietnamese S-75 batteries. Ryan Aeronautical took the basic Model 147N, added twin pods under its wing for scattering radar-spoofing foil chaff and tweaked its control system for medium-altitude flying.

The idea was for several of these Model 147NAs and improved Model 147NCs to launch before the fighters, laying down chaff in corridors as a kind of protective wall for the fighters.

The idea was sound, but lacking drone experience, TAC struggled to implement it. The drones were ready, but the command was not. In a series of decisions starting in May 1968, President Johnson limited, then halted, the US bombardment of North Vietnam.

Soon there weren't any major fighter-bomber operations for the Model 147NA/NCs to support. Tactical Air Command never flew an operational mission with its Lightning Bugs.

The US Navy did only slightly better.

Model 147H-18 was one of several high-flying H-model Lightning Bugs that crashed or were shot down over China in 1968. The Chinese government circulated this photo of H-18's remains under the caption 'Wipe Out the US Air Bandits!' Despite the high-profile shoot-downs, the Model 147H still boasted a better return rate – 64 percent – than did many of the low-altitude Lightning Bug variants. In any event, sacrificing a few Model 147s was preferable to losing manned U-2 spy planes. (*Teledyne Ryan photo courtesy of the San Diego Air and Space Museum Archive*)

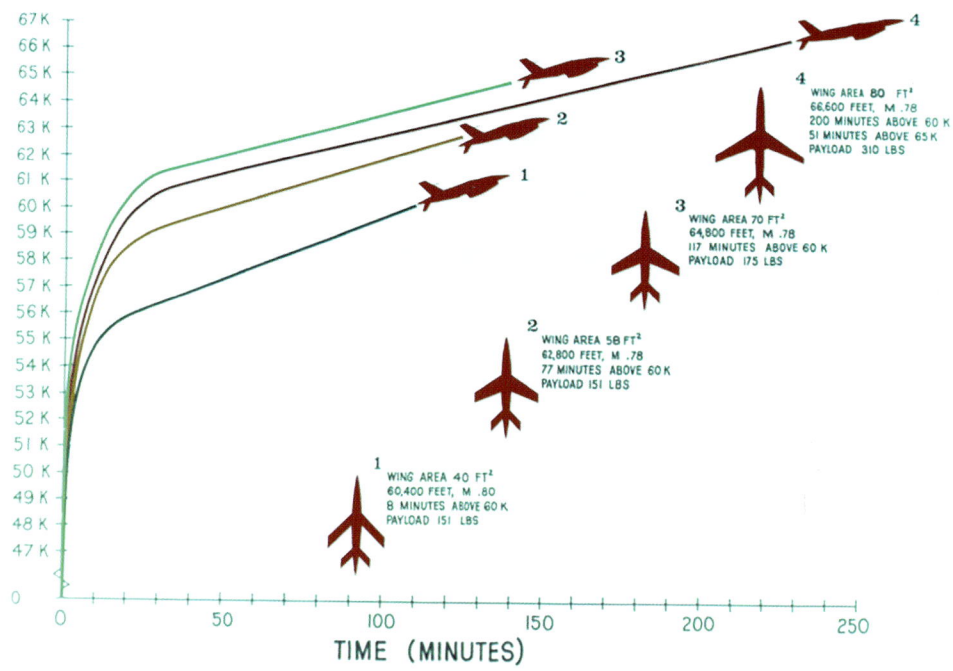

A Ryan Aeronautical chart depicting the climb and altitude performance of different Model 147 drone types. Variants with 40ft-square wings – including the C, D, NP, NRE, NA, NC and SK – were optimized for low-altitude operations, so their poor performance up high should come as no surprise. Ryan Aeronautical didn't actually build Model 147s with 58 or 70 sq ft wings, but it did field several variants with an 80 sq ft wing, including the E, F, G and J. The Models 147H, T, TE and TF had an even bigger 114 sq ft wing. (*Teledyne Ryan photo courtesy of the San Diego Air and Space Museum Archive*)

The Model 147S was a better low-level performer than the earlier Model 147J. Its smaller wing was stiffer and allowed for a smoother ride. In place of the finicky barometric low-altitude control system, the Model 147S had the new 'multiple altitude control system' (MACS). The S-model Lightning Bug also swapped out the J's two-camera set-up for a single panoramic camera that returned some truly remarkable images. One Model 147S snapped a series of photos of a V-750 missile flying alongside the drone right before exploding. Incredibly, the drone survived the close encounter with its biggest killer. (*US Air Force photo*)

The Model 147S was more survivable than earlier low-altitude Lightning Bugs. MACS had three settings, allowing a Model 147S to climb as high as 20,000ft and dive as low as 1,000ft during a mission. Frequent altitude changes helped the drone to zoom *over* anti-aircraft gunfire and *under* surface-to-air missiles. One lucky S-model Lightning Bug snapped a series of photos of a V-750 missile flying alongside the drone right before exploding. (*US Air Force photo*)

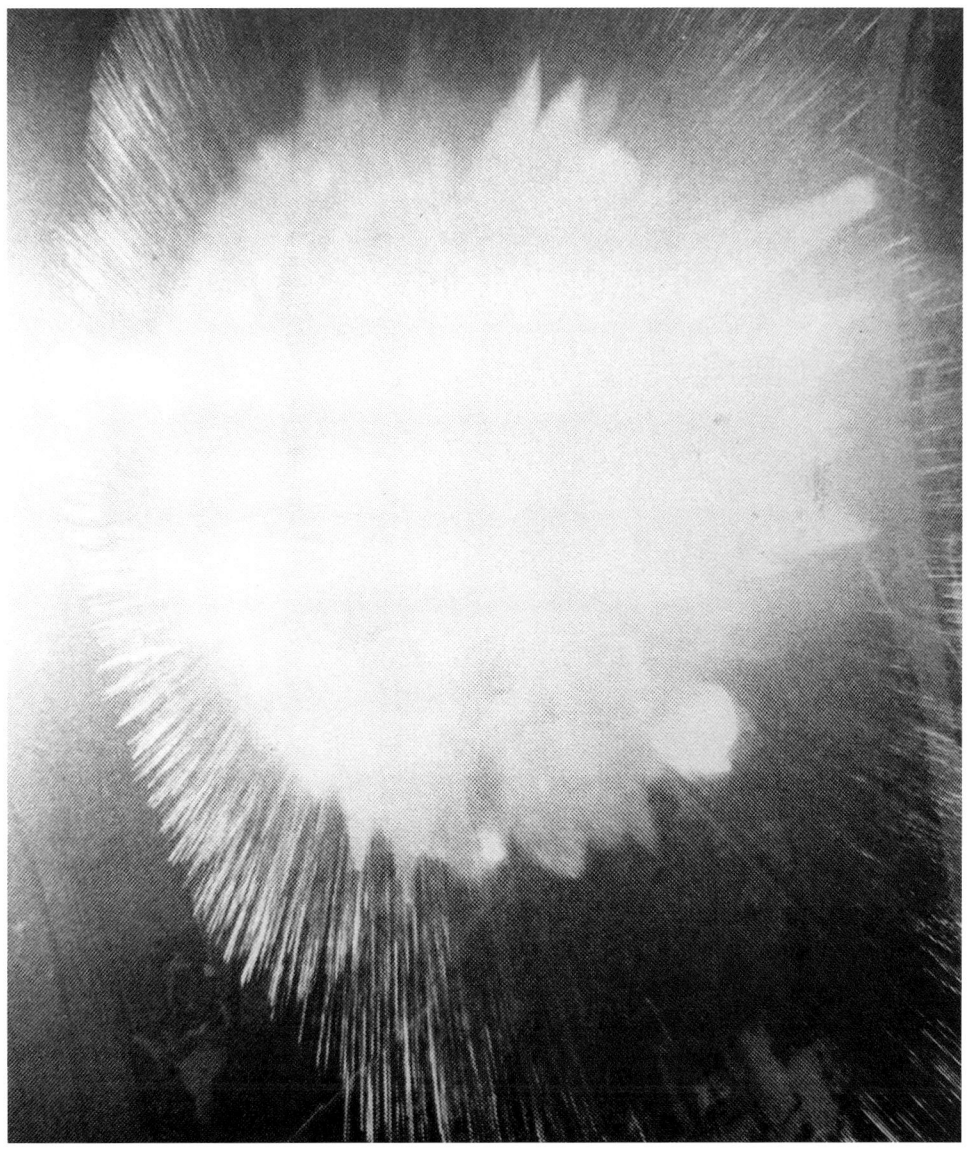

The Model 147SC, which flew its first front-line missions in January 1969, was the fourth production variant of the Model 147S. Deployed under the US Air Force's 'Buffalo Hunter' initiative, the Model 147SC inarguably was the most important Lightning Bug variant. Of the hundreds of Model 147S drones the Air Force acquired, most were Model 147SCs. The variant flew nearly half of all Lightning Bug missions. The four longest-serving Lightning Bugs were Model 147SCs, most notably 'Tom Cat', which completed sixty-eight missions compared to just three missions for the typical Lightning Bug.

The Model 147SC with the nickname 'Tom Cat' flew a record sixty-eight missions over North Vietnam before enemy gunners finally shot it down over Hanoi on September 25, 1974. Tom Cat's survival was remarkable. The US military in all bought more than 1,000 Model 147s. Each on average completed fewer than four operational sorties before crashing, getting shot down or otherwise being written off. (*Teledyne Ryan photo courtesy of the San Diego Air and Space Museum Archive*)

San Diego artist Robert Watts, Ryan Aeronautical's lead illustrator from the mid-1960s through the mid-1970s, produced this striking portrait of one of the longest-lived Model 147s, a low-flying SC model that completed sixty-eight missions compared to just three for the typical Lightning Bug. 'Tom Cat' finally fell to enemy air defenses in September 1974. (*Teledyne Ryan art courtesy of the San Diego Air and Space Museum Archive*)

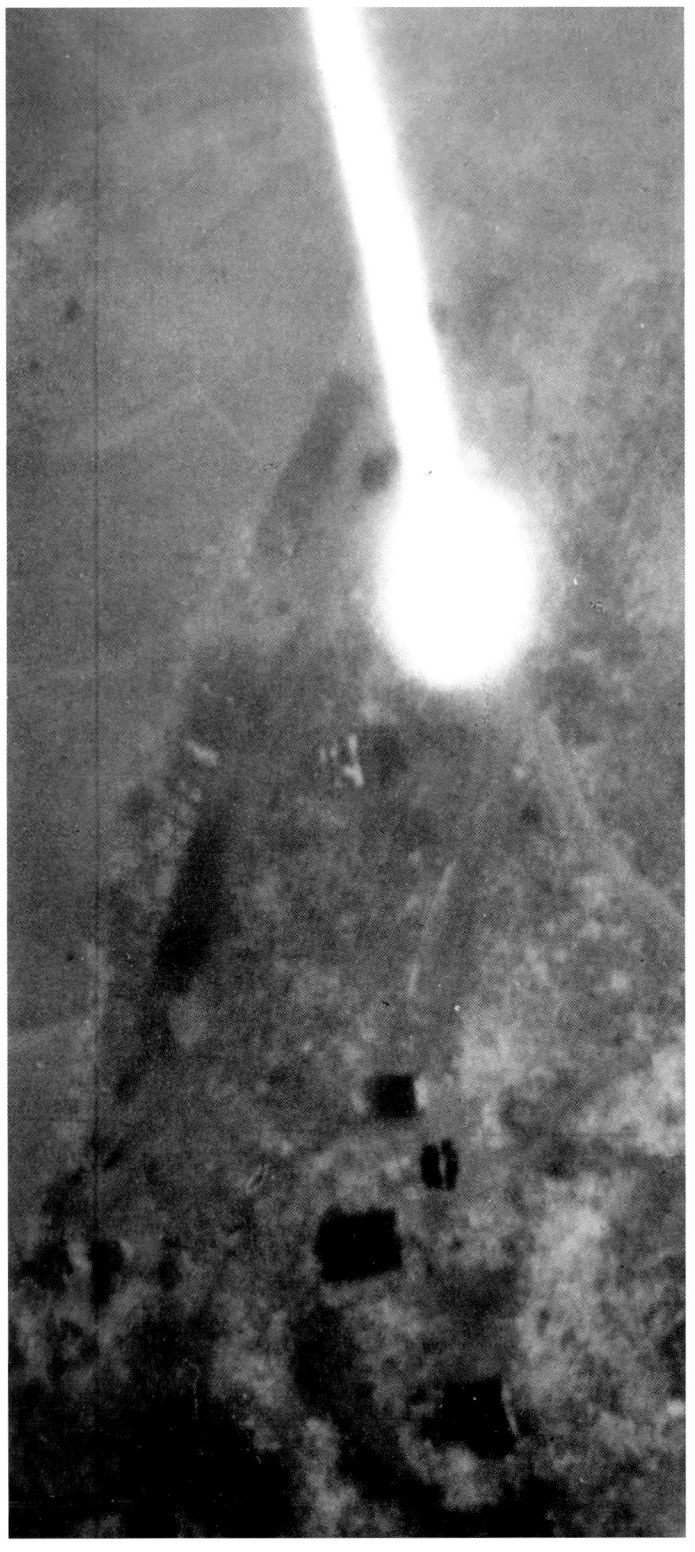

On December 19, 1968 Model 147SRE-2 snapped a photo of a V-750 missile that barely missed the drone. 'The SAM passed close enough to the camera window that it completely burned out that frame of imagery,' said Ryan Aeronautical engineer Ed Christian. (*US Air Force photo*)

The Model 147T, a variant of the Model 147H with a more powerful engine, could climb as high as 75,000ft. The Model 147T was the basis of the Model 147TE that Ryan Aeronautical developed specifically for recce flights along the border of North Korea. A Model 147T is pictured here following a landing on rough terrain during testing in 1968. (*Teledyne Ryan photo courtesy of the San Diego Air and Space Museum Archive*)

To meet the demand for intelligence on North Korea, Ryan Aeronautical proposed to modify the Model 147T, a variant of the Model 147H with a more powerful engine, to carry the same kind of ELINT receivers that were carried by the much larger, manned EC-121 spy plane. The Model 147TE would also have a real-time data-link that would allow it to beam raw data straight to a ground station. The idea was for the Model 147TEs to fly along the periphery of North Korea, feeding intelligence on North Korean forces straight to the National Security Agency. The military gave the Model 147TEs' mission the code-name 'Combat Dawn'. The Model 147TEs flew from OL-16 at Osan Air Base in South Korea for three years starting in January 1970. In all, OL-16 launched 268 Combat Dawn missions for a 91 percent return rate. (*Teledyne Ryan photo courtesy of the San Diego Air and Space Museum Archive*)

Starting in 1975, the US Air Force modified forty-seven surviving Model 147NCs with improved electronic countermeasures including active radar-jammers and chaff-dispensers. The service bought an additional sixteen of these so-called Model 255s but never actually deployed them for front-line use. The Model 255s went into storage in 1979. (*Teledyne Ryan photo courtesy of the San Diego Air and Space Museum Archive*)

# Chapter Thirteen

The Navy was a big user of Ryan Aeronautical target drones, and Navy carrier battle groups operating in the Gulf of Tonkin borrowed imagery from OL-20's Lightning Bugs. By 1967 the Navy had decided it wanted recce drones of its own.

At first, the fleet wanted the Lightning Bug as a sort of fast-acting anti-cruise missile platform. During the Six-Day War between Israel and its Arab neighbors in June 1967, Egyptian forces used a Soviet-made Styx cruise missile to sink the Israeli destroyer *Elath*, killing forty-nine sailors.

The sinking chilled US Navy leaders. They imagined Soviet missiles overwhelming American ships in the event that the Cold War turned hot. While ship-launched surface-to-air missiles were getting better by the month, these were defensive systems. The Navy wanted an offensive weapon that could strike Soviet ships before they could launch their own anti-ship missiles.

The Navy asked Ryan Aeronautical to develop a version of the Lightning Bug that could launch from a ship at sea while carrying an explosive warhead as heavy as 1,000lb and crash, kamikaze-style, into enemy vessels. Ryan Aeronautical dubbed the anti-ship drone the 'Model 248'.

The anti-ship Lightning Bug required advancements in several subsystems. It needed a more powerful rocket booster to allow it to launch from the deck of a warship. It needed a highly accurate low-altitude radar altimeter. It required a TV camera in the nose that could feed a live image to a shipboard operator who could steer the drone to its aiming-point.

Between 1968 and 1971 the fleet separately tested the booster, the altimeter and the remote-control system on lightly-modified Q-2Cs. During one test off the California coast in September 1971, the drone flew so close to its target ship that it clipped a wire and exploded.

By 1971 the Model 248 was ready for a major investment, but the Navy demurred. The fleet also had been developing the Harpoon anti-ship cruise missile. Faced with a choice, the Navy opted to spend its dwindling development budget on the smaller and fully autonomous Harpoon.

The Navy got further with recce drones. Around the same time the fleet launched development of the Model 248, it also began integrating unarmed Model 147s on aircraft carriers.

Carrier air wings didn't operate aircraft large enough to launch the Model 147. They'd have to blast off directly from a carrier's deck. While the military routinely launched Q-2C targets from land, the operational Model 147 was strictly air-launched.

So Ryan Aeronautical got to work modifying ten Model 147SCs for deck-launch, adding a 15ft-span wing and strapping a small rocket booster to the drones to help get them up to speed. A test launch in San Diego ended in embarrassment for Ryan Aeronautical when the drone flipped over and exploded not far from a watching admiral.

Trials moved to the carrier USS *Bennington* sailing off Southern California. The Second World War-vintage flattop was an anti-submarine vessel. Its air wing included helicopters and slow-flying, propeller-driven sub-hunters. The pace of launches and landings was slow compared to the hectic activity aboard the attack carriers on Yankee Station in the Gulf of Tonkin.

The Navy laid down an extra steel plate on one of *Bennington*'s elevators in order to deflect the blast from the drone's rocket booster. The first at-sea test was only slightly less embarrassing than was the ground test. The booster fired but the drone's engine never fully spun up. The drone lobbed itself into the ocean off *Bennington*'s starboard side.

Subsequent tests went better. A Ryan Aeronautical team on October 14, 1969 embarked on the attack carrier USS *Ranger* with three Model 147SKs. The carrier set sail for Yankee Station, pausing near Hawaii and again off the Philippines for training. The stop-overs also afforded the contractors an opportunity to bring aboard additional drones.

The plan was for a drone to launch from *Ranger*'s deck and recover by popping a 'chute and descending into the sea near the carrier, which would dispatch a helicopter to fish the drone out of the water. There was no time to train the Navy 'copter crews on the MARS method of recovery.

Operators aboard one of the carrier's E-2 radar early-warning planes would send commands via radio to steer the Lightning Bug to a checkpoint where the drone's internal navigation system would take over.

Problems abounded. The carrier was too crowded and too busy for the sudden addition of a new and complex system. The E-2 crews were unfamiliar with the Model 147. The carrier tended to drift a few miles from its target station, skewing the drone's navigational programming. The Lightning Bug crew had to launch its drone after *Ranger* launched a strike package and recover the drone before the package returned, leaving no room for error.

Of the first five front-line sorties in November 1969, just one was successful. The success rate picked up as 1969 turned to 1970. Model 147SK-5 in particular proved reliable and lucky ... until it wasn't.

On February 10, 1970 the drone launched from *Ranger* on its ninth and final mission. The E-2 crew sent command signals to the Lightning Bug, apparently without realizing that, in fact, they didn't even have the drone on their radar scopes.

The admiral aboard *Ranger* grew frustrated. 'Recover it!' he commanded. The operators pressed the button commanding the drone to pop its recovery parachute. As far as anyone knew, SK-5 was floating down to Earth, but no one knew *where*.

A few days later the Honolulu *Star Bulletin* broke the news. The Chinese government had 'shot down' an American drone over Hainan Island. In fact, the Chinese had simply snatched up the drone after it gently parachuted to the ground on *Ranger*'s command. The Lightning Bug enjoyed a period of notoriety as a major subject of Chinese propaganda.

Missions in April 1970 were by and large successful. The Lightning Bugs returned to *Ranger* with clear photos of SAM sites, anti-aircraft artillery batteries, railways, highways and bridges.

*Ranger* flew her twenty-eighth and last Lightning Bug mission on May 10, 1970. The drone survived its run over North Vietnam but its recovery parachute failed to deploy. It disappeared beneath the Pacific waves. Ryan Aeronautical later concluded that saltwater corrosion had damaged the 'chute mechanism.

With that, all the Model 147SKs had been shot down, crashed, sank or delivered themselves into Chinese hands. The Navy declined to order more.

The consensus at Ryan Aeronautical was that the SKs would have worked better if the Navy had invested the time and money to develop a carrier-compatible mothership plane and a MARS that worked with fleet helicopters. 'The Navy got what it paid for,' Weaver said.

Around the same time the Navy was flying its last operational Lightning Bug sorties, the Air Force was making some major changes to its own drone ops. Mortar and rocket attacks on Bien Hoa had been escalating. In July 1970 the 100th Strategic Reconnaissance Wing, formerly the 4080th SRW, for the fourth time relocated its drone detachment, this time to U Tapao Air Base in southern Thailand.

U Tapao would also soon host a massive contingent of B-52 bombers, whose apocalyptic missions in late 1972 signaled the end of America's long, bloody involvement in Vietnam.

By 1967 the US Navy had decided it wanted drones of its own. At first, the fleet envisioned the Lightning Bug as a sort of fast-acting anti-cruise-missile platform. While ship-launched surface-to-air missiles were getting better by the month, these were defensive systems. The Navy wanted an offensive weapon that could strike Soviet ships before they could launch their own anti-ship missiles. The fleet eventually canceled the anti-ship drone in favor of the smaller, more efficient Harpoon anti-ship cruise missile. However, the US Air Force revived the concept of a weaponized Model 147 in 1970. The armed Model 234A never flew in combat. (*Teledyne Ryan photo courtesy of the San Diego Air and Space Museum Archive*)

Trials of the carrier-capable Model 147SK in mid-1969 moved to the carrier USS *Bennington* sailing off Southern California. The Second World War-vintage flattop was an anti-submarine vessel. The Navy laid down an extra steel plate on one of *Bennington*'s elevators in order to deflect the blast from the drone's rocket booster. (*Teledyne Ryan art courtesy of the San Diego Air and Space Museum Archive*)

Trials of the Model 147SK took place on the carrier USS *Bennington* sailing off Southern California in October 1969. During the first at-sea test, the booster fired but the drone's engine never fully spun up. The drone lobbed itself into the ocean off *Bennington*'s starboard side. (*Teledyne Ryan photo courtesy of the San Diego Air and Space Museum Archive*)

# Chapter Fourteen

On July 9, 1967 Navy commander Edward Martin was in the cockpit of his A-4C attack plane speeding toward Hanoi. Some 15 miles from the city center, the S-75 batteries opened fire. A V-750 exploded just 250ft in front of the compact, single-engine fighter.

Martin flew directly into the blast. 'That was the start of my five-and-a-half years as an unwilling guest of the North Vietnamese,' Martin said later. A week later he was in his cell at Hoa Lo Prison in Hanoi, in his own words a 'crumbling heap of humanity tied up in ropes and lying near unconsciousness on the floor.'

An air-raid siren wailed. Anti-aircraft gunners opened up. Prison guards and interrogators raced for cover. After twenty minutes, calm returned. The prison staff resumed their work. Martin's own guards were 'more than a little angry' when they returned.

That's when Martin heard the distinctive whine of a Model 147 recce drone. He knew the sound because he'd shot at Q-2s in training in 1959. During a mission over the Gulf of Tonkin prior to his shoot-down and capture, he'd seen, although obviously not heard, Lightning Bugs going about their business.

The North Vietnamese gunners opened fire again. Martin's interrogator later claimed, without proof, that the gunners had shot down the drone. Martin wasn't convinced.

Over the following years Martin had many encounters with Lightning Bugs as they flew ahead of manned bombers in order to spot targets, or followed behind the bombers to assess the effectiveness of a raid.

'One thing that impressed me most about the pilotless recce aircraft was the relative degree of impunity with which they intruded upon North Vietnamese air space,' Martin recalled. 'When a strike force of bombers and attack planes came in, there was always an alert, but when a single 147 Firebee … came in fast and low they wouldn't draw an alert.'

More than once, Martin and his fellow prisoners were outside bathing and washing their clothes when a Lightning Bug appeared overhead. The guards excitedly would usher the prisoners inside then open fire with their small arms, never hitting the speedy little drones.

In the spring of 1968, after the North Vietnamese had moved Martin to a different prison, one known as 'The Zoo', a Model 147 approached the prison complex at high speed. Radar-aimed anti-aircraft guns opened fire and scored multiple hits on the drone but failed to destroy it.

Martin said his guard was 'absolutely horrified'. The guard tried to shoo Martin inside but he and his fellow prisoners refused to go. 'I remember we were all elated, so much so that they dragged me out for special treatment as I was the senior officer at The Zoo. They reprimanded me for my bad attitude because I had smiled when one of the "spy planes", as they called them, intruded upon the Vietnamese people.'

Lightning Bug missions continued even after President Johnson ordered a second halt to bombing in North Vietnam starting in April 1968. Johnson hoped the pause would bring the North Vietnamese to the negotiating table and also give his vice president Hubert Humphrey an electoral boost in that fall's presidential election.

The bombing pause didn't work on either count. Republican Richard Nixon, a former vice president, defeated Humphrey.

Although Nixon extended the bombing pause, allowing only infrequent retaliatory raids, there were no diplomatic breakthroughs. For four years, drones and a few manned recce planes were the only American aircraft Martin heard over his prison. 'They were about the only thing that did lift our morale during those years,' Martin said.

The North Vietnamese released Martin in 1973. In April of that year, he dropped by Ryan Aeronautical in San Diego to tell company workers all about the years he spent staring into the sky at passing Lightning Bugs.

Nixon resumed major bombing of North Vietnam in April 1972 in response to a series of North Vietnamese offensives. American air power in South Vietnam had atrophied during the four-year bombing pause. Now it quickly bulked up.

The Navy surged five aircraft carriers to the Gulf of Tonkin. Strategic Air Command deployed 152 eight-engine B-52D and B-52G bombers to Guam and another 54 to U Tapao airfield in Thailand to complement a huge force of fighter-bombers flying from South Vietnam and Thailand.

Model 147s had never stopped flying during the four-year bombing pause, of course, but the resumption of air-raids did alter the demand signal for unmanned operations. Model 147s would fly bomb-damage assessment missions to photograph the devastation that mass formations of B-52s sowed across North Vietnam.

The Air Force also revived the Navy's concept for an armed drone. Ryan Aeronautical actually had been tinkering with the armed Model 234A since at least 1970, spurred by the Pentagon's alarm over the rapid advancement of Soviet air-defense networks. The Air Force hoped that drones firing guided missiles or dropping guided bombs could help clear a path through the air defenses to allow manned aircraft to safely pass.

The Model 234A in fact was a Model 147S with the latest altitude-control system plus a TV camera in the nose. The camera fed live video to a remote operator who could control the vehicle via a joystick linked to the drone's flight-control surfaces. OL-20 would operate TV-equipped Model 147SC/TVs starting in June 1972.

Tests of the Model 234A focused on the drone's ability to carry and fire the TV-guided AGM-65 Maverick anti-tank missile. The missile itself relayed to the drone controller the image from its nose-mounted camera. So in effect the same control team separately could steer the missile-carrying drone and – once launched – the missile itself.

An October 1971 test was a smashing success. The drone approached within 3 miles of the target, at which point the Maverick's own seeker could clearly see the aiming-point. The operators launched the missile. Nine seconds later it scored a direct hit.

At that moment, the Air Force in theory possessed an armed drone that was capable of striking targets with high precision while under remote control. Notably, this achievement came thirty years to the month before the service's historic first lethal drone strike in Afghanistan, using a decidedly less survivable propeller-driven platform firing *the same basic type of missile* that the Model 234A carried in 1971.

With the resumption of bombing in Vietnam, the Air Force wanted to deploy armed drones as soon as possible. 'Everyone wanted to cut down the number of guests at the Hanoi Hilton,' Ryan Aeronautical employee Bill Helmich explained.

In fact, the Vietnam War would end before the armed Lightning Bugs could join the action, but Model 147s participated in other ways in the belated escalation that preceded the abrupt and bloody end of the conflict for the United States.

The Air Force wanted to complement its lethal raids in 1972 with intensive propaganda efforts. The service for years had been scattering paper leaflets – millions of them – across North Vietnam in an effort to win hearts and change minds.

Some of the early leaflets were just long statements from President Johnson extolling the reader to choose peace. Others depicted American warplanes and the damage they could inflict. Some mocked communist leaders. Some included photos of North Vietnamese dead.

Operation FIELD GOAL, which ran between July 1972 and January 1973, involved F-4 fighters, C-130 transports, B-52 bombers and Model 147 drones dropping 94 million leaflets per month for a grand total of 661 million scraps of paper.

Tactical Air Command's chaff-dispensing Model 147NCs were perfect for the role. The command simply swapped out radar-foiling metal strips for paper leaflets. However, TAC wasn't ready to set up its own drone operation in South-East Asia.

The command transferred at least three Model 147NCs to the SAC operation at U Tapao.

The 'bullshit bombers', as the Lightning Bug team called the leaflet-dispensers, flew twenty-nine missions between July and December 1972.

However, the most important missions the Lightning Bug force flew in mid-1972 aimed to duplicate the accomplishments of 1965 and '66, when Model 147Es captured the radar and fuzing signals from North Vietnamese S-75 batteries.

Those helped the Air Force to develop radar-jammers specifically for defeating the S-75. Six years later North Vietnam had acquired new Fan Song fire-control radars for its deadly SAMs. The upgraded Fan Songs boasted more and better antennas for more precise and jam-proof control of the V-750 missile.

The Air Force needed to update its jammers. It again turned to drones to capture the signals.

The task was urgent. Strategic Air Command was spooling up its B-52 wings for mass attacks on North Vietnamese targets, including military and industrial sites in and around Hanoi that enjoyed the protection of what was then the world's densest air-defense network, which at the time included no fewer than twenty-one S-75 sites. The command called the operation 'Linebacker II'.

With the resumption of major bombing in Vietnam in 1971, the Air Force wanted to deploy armed drones as soon as possible. 'Everyone wanted to cut down the number of guests at the Hanoi Hilton,' Ryan Aeronautical employee Bill Helmich explained. In fact, the Vietnam War would end before the armed Lightning Bugs could join the action. (*Teledyne Ryan photo courtesy of the San Diego Air and Space Museum Archive*)

Ryan Aeronautical began tinkering with the armed Model 234A around 1970, spurred on by the Pentagon's alarm over the rapid advancement of Soviet air-defense networks. The Model 234A in fact was a Model 147S with the latest altitude-control system plus a TV camera in the nose. The Air Force hoped that drones firing guided missiles or dropping guided bombs could help clear a path through the air defenses to allow manned aircraft to safely pass. (*Teledyne Ryan photo courtesy of the San Diego Air and Space Museum Archive*)

Tests of the Model 234A focused on the drone's ability to carry and fire the TV-guided AGM-65 anti-tank missile. The missile itself relayed to the drone controller the image from its nose-mounted camera. So in effect the same control team could separately steer the missile-carrying drone and – once launched – the missile itself. An October 1971 test was a smashing success. The drone approached to within 3 miles of the target, at which point the Maverick's own seeker could clearly see the aiming-point. The operators launched the missile. Nine seconds later it scored a direct hit. (*Teledyne Ryan art courtesy of the San Diego Air and Space Museum Archive*)

The armed Model 234A in fact was a Model 147S with the latest altitude-control system plus a TV camera in the nose. The US Air Force experimented with different weapons, including the Hobo guided missile, the Shrike radar-homing missile and, pictured here, a Maverick anti-tank missile and an air-retarded unguided bomb in a mixed load-out. (*Teledyne Ryan photo courtesy of the San Diego Air and Space Museum Archive*)

A US Air Force B-52D takes off from Guam for a Linebacker II raid over North Vietnam in December 1972. For the operation Strategic Air Command deployed 152 B-52Ds and B-52Gs to Guam and another 54 to U Tapao airfield in Thailand to complement a huge force of fighter-bombers flying from South Vietnam and Thailand. Fifteen of the bombers were shot down in eleven days of raids, all by SAMs. (*US Air Force photo*)

# Chapter Fifteen

SAC crunched the numbers and came up with a precise plan for carpet-bombing Hanoi. B-52s would time their take-offs from U Tapao and Guam so that they arrived at their 'initial points' outside Hanoi while under the cover of darkness.

Flying in three-plane formations at an altitude of 30,000ft or higher, the 159ft-long bombers would drive straight into Hanoi without changing altitude, jinking or maneuvering at all. The idea was for the three bombers to cover each other with their powerful AN/ALT-22 jammers.

After dropping their loads of up to 108 500lb and 750lb bombs, the B-52s would turn away from Hanoi as a formation and head back to base.

It was the turn that most worried SAC planners. The maneuver could open gaps in the overlapping jamming coverage, since the bombers' emitters mostly projected forward and backward. The turn also boosted the bomber formation's radar signature. Finally, it slowed the bombers by as much as 100 miles per hour as they turned into the wind.

Needless to say, if the jammers failed, the bombers were in big trouble. Anticipating the problem, in September 1972 the Air Force sent Weaver to U Tapao with a few old Model 147Hs carrying electronic sniffers.

Weaver launched four sorties under the auspices of Operation COMPASS COOKIE. Three V-750s targeted the drone. Right before the missiles exploded, the Lightning Bug transmitted its life-saving data to the C-130 mothership. The Air Force quickly modified the AN/ALT-22s on all the B-52Ds and around half of the B-52Gs that carried the jammer. The rest of the G-models packed older AN/ALT-6Bs.

The B-52s launched for the first Linebacker II raids on the afternoon of December 18, 1972. Eighty-seven B-52s roared off the runways at Guam. Forty-two departed U Tapao. Together they hauled almost 14,000 bombs.

The North Vietnamese air defenders opened up with everything they had: 200 SAMs arced into the sky. At the peak of the aerial battle, forty missiles were in the air at the same time. Three B-52s fell to the ground in flames, including one of the Gs with an AN/ALT-6B instead of the latest AN/ALT-22. Two were hit during or after their outbound turn.

On the second day of Linebacker II, SAC authorized evasive maneuvers. Some 93 bombers took off, and 180 SAMs rose up to meet them. No hits.

Day three was a bloodbath for the Americans. Six of the ninety bombers were shot down, including four Gs without the modified jammer. Three fell while making their turn toward home.

By day four the trend was clear. The turn was deadly, so SAC plotted new egress routes that allowed bombers flying from Thailand to continue straight ahead, out over the Gulf of Tonkin before making a leisurely southward jog.

SAC also realized that the bombers without the latest jammer were unacceptably vulnerable. On day four the command only launched B-52Ds, and it authorized the B-52 wings to add AN/ALT-28 jammers to their bombers. The AN/ALT-28 specifically targeted the S-75's downlink, the radio signal connecting the battery to an airborne missile.

SAC lost two B-52s on day four. Lieutenant Colonel Bill Conlee was the electronic-warfare officer on one of those doomed B-52s. 'Between I.P. and bomb-release point, ten SAMs were fired in the vicinity of Blue Cell,' he recalled.

'At bombs away we were bracketed by two SAMs, one going off below us and to the left, the second exploding above us and to the right. Shrapnel cracked the pilot's outer window glass, started fires in the left wing and wounded Lieutenant Colonel [John] Yuill, the pilot; Lieutenant Colonel [Louis] Bernasconi, the radar navigator; Lieutenant [William] Mayall, the navigator; and myself. We also experienced a rapid decompression and loss of electrical power.'

'Shortly after this, with the fire worsening, Lieutenant Colonel Yuill gave the emergency bail-out signal via the alarm light and I ejected from the aircraft. During free-fall, two more SAMs passed me, and I attempted to look for our aircraft, but was unable to see it.'

Conlee descended under fire from North Vietnamese gunners and, badly hurt, spent a year in prison in Hanoi. His crewmates all survived ejection and joined him in captivity. In 11 days of raids ending on December 29, 1972, SAC launched 729 B-52 sorties. The North Vietnamese in return fired around 900 surface-to-air missiles.

Fifteen B-52s were shot down – all by SAMs – and several others were damaged beyond repair. Eighteen crew died. Fifteen went missing. The bombers in return inflicted heavy damage on North Vietnamese military and industrial facilities. In late December a Model 147SC penetrated Hanoi's air defenses and snapped a photograph of the city's thermal power plant.

A November 1972 photo, also taken by a Lightning Bug, revealed an intact and functioning facility. The December photo showed … craters.

American prisoners of war in Hanoi had front-row seats to the B-52 raids and the drone damage-assessment sorties. 'It was spectacular,' Navy captain James Mulligan said of the bomber attacks. 'I knew the war would end when the B-52s came.' Mulligan recalled smiling up at a passing Lightning Bug, hoping it would snap a clear photo of his face.

Mulligan was right, in a sense. He was also wrong. For all the damage it inflicted, the Linebacker II campaign did not turn the tide of the war. In January 1973 the Nixon administration cajoled the South Vietnamese government under President Nguyen Van Thieu into joining the United States and North Vietnam in signing the Paris Peace Accords.

The ceasefire ended America's nine-year war in Vietnam. As many as 3.6 million people died, including more than 58,000 Americans. In nearly a decade of air operations, US forces lost 3,744 airplanes, 5,607 helicopters and 578 drones. North Vietnam claimed its S-75 batteries shot down more than 1,000 enemy aircraft. The United States confirmed just 200 of those shoot-downs.

The fighting didn't actually end in 1973, of course. Following months of steady advances against South Vietnamese forces, in late April 1975 the North Vietnamese army launched its final assault on Saigon. Tens of thousands of Americans and Vietnamese working with and for the South Vietnamese government fled in boats and helicopters.

On the morning of April 30, 1975 a North Vietnamese tank crashed through the gate of Saigon's Independence Palace, the seat of President Duong Van Minh's crumbling government. Minh and his advisors sat and waited for communist troops to accept their surrender.

The war was over. Lightning Bugs continued to launch from U Tapao in Thailand and Osan in South Korea for a few weeks, but an era of intervention was ending. Americans were coming home. The last drone mission from U Tapao took place on April 30, 1975. The last flight out of Osan was on June 3, 1975.

The 100th SRW shuttered its Lightning Bug detachment. Scores of Model 147s survived. The Air Force shipped the war-weary drones home and stored them at bases across the United States, in particular at Warner Robins Air Force Base in Georgia and Hill Air Force Base in Utah.

Aiming to shift drone operations to Europe, Tactical Air Command briefly tinkered with an improved version of the armed Lightning Bug, but the command cooled to the idea following several studies and experiments.

One 1973 study estimated that during wartime NATO would need eighteen drone flights per day to meet recce and defense-suppression requirements. That in turn would require eight DC-130 motherships and twenty-five MARS helicopters.

Maintaining a single wing to undertake these flights would cost $35 million annually, the study found. By comparison, a wing of F-4E fighter-bombers cost just $25 million and could daily generate *hundreds* of sorties.

TAC also worried that Soviet fighters would gobble up Lightning Bugs at a rate that North Vietnam's meager air force could never achieve.

Then there were the treaty implications. The Strategic Arms Limitation Treaty II, which Soviet and American diplomats had been negotiating since 1972, included language limiting both countries' deployments of cruise missiles.

As for the treaty, the term 'cruise missile' covered all 'unmanned, self-propelled, guided weapon-delivery vehicles which sustain flight through the use of aerodynamic lift over most of their flight path and which are flight-tested from or deployed on aircraft.'

The Lightning Bug was, by that definition, a cruise missile, and a threat to the key arms-control treaty. TAC's drone group disbanded in 1979. It would be nearly two decades before the low-intensity wars in the Balkans, and later Afghanistan and Iraq, helped to create the conditions for a drone resurgence.

Two decades of hard work selling, developing and deploying drones had a profound and tragic impact on one of the central figures in the Lightning Bug's story.

Schwanhausser's high stress levels may have contributed to his heavy drinking and drug use. He suffered a heart attack in 1968 and nine years later nearly died of an overdose of alcohol and lithium. Schwanhausser married and divorced three times. Yet even that tragedy had a happy ending. In 2003 at the age of 72, Schwanhausser traveled to Thailand for gender-reassignment surgery. She returned home to Michigan as Bobbi Swan and died fifteen years later.

When a newspaper reporter asked Swan why she hadn't changed sex earlier, she was blunt. 'Priorities,' she said. 'My priorities were airplanes and getting established in the airplane business. Obviously, that was a man's business.'

Starting in 1972, the low-flying Model 147SD was one of the last Lightning Bug variants to see combat over North Vietnam. The SD carried external underwing tanks to extend its range and also boasted a more accurate navigation system compared to other Lightning Bugs, as well as a new cooling system to handle South-East Asia's extreme temperatures. The Model 147SD also formed the basis of an Israeli version of the Lightning Bug that saw combat during the 1973 Yom Kippur War. (*Teledyne Ryan photo courtesy of the San Diego Air and Space Museum Archive*)

Aiming to shift drone operations to Europe in the aftermath of the Vietnam War, Tactical Air Command briefly tinkered with an improved version of the armed Lightning Bug. However, one 1973 study estimated that during wartime NATO would need eighteen drone flights per day to meet recce and defense-suppression requirements. That in turn would require eight DC-130 motherships and twenty-five MARS helicopters. Maintaining a single wing to undertake these flights would cost $35 million annually, the study found. By comparison, a wing of F-4E fighter-bombers cost just $25 million and could daily generate *hundreds* of sorties. Pictured here is a scale model of an armed Lightning Bug undergoing wind-tunnel testing in 1972. (*Teledyne Ryan photo courtesy of the San Diego Air and Space Museum Archive*)

On the morning of April 30, 1975 a North Vietnamese tank crashed through the gate of Saigon's Independence Palace, the seat of President Duong Van Minh's crumbling government. The Vietnam War was over. Lightning Bugs continued to launch from U Tapao in Thailand and Osan in South Korea for a few weeks, but Americans were coming home. The last drone mission from U Tapao took place on April 30, 1975. The last flight out of Osan was on June 3, 1975. A South Korea-based Model 147TE is pictured here following a parachute recovery near Osan. (*Teledyne Ryan photo courtesy of the San Diego Air and Space Museum Archive*)

Ryan Aeronautical target drones continued to perform a vital function in US Air Force training decades after the Lightning Bug flew its last combat sortie over Vietnam. In this photo from October 1982, a 1970-model Fire Bee II drone leaves its launch pad at Tyndall Air Force Base in Florida during a William Tell air-to-air gunnery exercise. (*US Defense Department photo by Technical Sergeant Frank Garzelnick*)

A DC-130H Hercules drone mothership carrying two Firebee target drones banks over the US Navy guided-missile cruiser USS *Chosin* during a test of the ship's Aegis anti-air warfare system in May 1991. The US Defense Department ended DC-130 operations in 2007, citing the high cost of supporting the aging planes, especially compared to the cheaper ground-launch method. (*US Air Force photo*)

Military Sealift Command dry-cargo and ammunition ship USNS *Charles Drew* launches a Northrop Grumman BQM-74E Chukar III target drone during exercise VALIANT SHIELD 2016 in September 2016. The BQM-74E is a development of the MQM-74A Chukar I, which first flew in 1964. The Navy since then has ordered thousands of Chukars as alternatives to Q-2Cs and other Ryan Aeronautical drones. Ironically, the Ryan Aeronautical drones became Northrop Grumman products starting in 1999, when Northrop acquired Ryan. (*US Navy photo by Mass Communication Specialist Second Class Diana Quinlan*)

# Chapter Sixteen

In mid-1966 the Air Force was feeling optimistic about drones. Brass in blue suits organized wresting control of UAV development from the NRO and Big Safari. The goal was to field a far- and high-flying drone specifically for penetrating deep into Chinese air space in order to survey the Lop Nor nuclear facility.

Air Force Systems Command believed, not without evidence, that Big Safari programs with their secrecy and special acquisitions rules encouraged non-competitive, sole-source contracts, and that in turn fostered unhealthy, cozy relationships between military managers and corporate executives.

Sole-source contracts and military-industry chumminess were the major ingredients for sloppy performance and cost overruns, in Systems Command's view. The Lightning Bug program, with its years of disastrous unreliability and sharp cost spikes, gave Systems Command all the evidence it needed to argue its case to top Air Force and Defense Department leaders.

By June 1966 the development coup was over. The 'Big' Air Force had won. Systems Command rather than the NRO and Big Safari would oversee the next drone program.

The Air Force asked North American Aviation and Ryan Aeronautical to compete for the production of 100 new 'Compass Arrow' recce drones that could fly as high as 80,000ft at a top speed of more than 600 miles per hour over a distance of 2,000 miles with a high degree of navigational accuracy and a payload of the latest long focal-length cameras.

The Air Force separately commissioned General Electric to produce a new engine for the drone: the J97.

Ryan Aeronautical pulled a classic trick and placed a $35-million bid that company leaders knew was too low and which would result in cost overruns. 'The 154 was a victim of too much optimism in the heat of a very tough competition to get the business,' Wagner noted.

The firm gave the Compass Arrow drone the internal designation 'Model 154'. Its creators chose the nickname 'Firefly'. Ryan Aeronautical put Schwanhausser in charge.

The 34ft-long drone featured a sharply-swept wing and all the high-tech features Ryan Aeronautical and the Air Force had developed for late-model Lightning Bugs:

contrail-suppression, jammers for defeating S-75 batteries, systems for automatic evasive maneuvers. The Lightning Bug had produced offspring.

Development was supposed to take just eighteen months but instead stretched out over five years. The total cost swelled to $250 million while the production order shrank to just twenty-eight airframes, eight of which were test models.

Even though Compass Arrow belonged to the Air Force and not the NRO, the program still maintained a high degree of secrecy.

Testing began in June 1968. A foul-up fourteen months later in August 1969 blew Compass Arrow's cover. A Firefly's control-surface actuator malfunctioned as the drone soared over the White Sands Missile Range in New Mexico. The malfunction triggered automatic emergency procedures. The Firefly cut its engine and popped its orange-and-white recovery parachute.

As the C-130 launch plane flew overhead, the drone floated down to a soft landing in a picnic area just inside the perimeter fence of the Los Alamos federal nuclear laboratory, close enough to adjacent residential neighborhoods for thousands of civilians to see it. Some took pictures.

Atomic Energy Commission area manager H. Jack Blackwell watched through his office window as the Firefly land nearby.

'I don't like it, I don't like it,' muttered Major Ken Beckner, the C-130's pilot.

Ryan Aeronautical employee Dale Weaver and another company man were aboard the C-130. The plane quickly diverted to Santa Fe. Weaver, his co-worker and the Air Force launch crew rented cars and sped back to Los Alamos.

Stopping for directions at a New Mexico Highway Patrol office, Weaver's crew ran into some very curious officers. 'I'm not going to tell you where it is until you tell me what it is,' one officer said.

News crews were already gathering along the lab fence when Weaver and company arrived to begin recovering the wayward drone. It would take them twenty-eight hours of work to disassemble the drone, crane it onto a rented truck, haul it to Santa Fe and load it onto the C-130.

Soon after the Firefly had touched down, Los Alamos workers helpfully had covered it with tarps, but the gesture was much too late.

Associated Press reporter Bill Stockton rushed out a dispatch citing Blackwell that appeared in newspapers in August. 'Reverberations from the thud of the graceful bird's landing on the northern New Mexico mountain plateau, 150 miles from White Sands, was felt all the way to Washington,' Stockton wrote.

Photos of the drone ended up at the office of the *Los Alamos Monitor* newspaper. Government agents pressed editor Markly McMahon to turn over the photos but he declined. 'It's not every day that you see a plane coming down on a big orange-and-white double parachute with a C-130 Air Force plane circling over the town.'

The Air Force had no choice but to confirm the Firefly's existence. A year later trade magazine *Aviation Week* published a story accurately detailing the Model 154's appearance and capabilities.

By 1970 things were not looking good for the Firefly. It didn't help that the drone had competition in the form of arguably the most famous manned spy plane that ever flew – the SR-71 Blackbird – as well as a super-fast drone that literally piggybacked on the Blackbird's success.

Lockheed designed the Blackbird from the wheels up, wrapping a titanium airframe around two J58 turbojets, then among the most powerful aircraft engines anywhere in the world.

The SR-71 was huge, exceeding 100ft in length and tipping the scales at 30 tons fully loaded. It could reach a top speed of almost 2,200 miles per hour and climb higher than 80,000ft.

However, that performance came at a cost. The SR-71 was outrageously pricey at a whopping $34 million in 1966. Like a B-2 stealth bomber is now or the Space Shuttle was in its day, the Blackbird was a national asset and an object of national pride.

The Air Force bought just fifty SR-71s and its variants. Twenty crashed, making heroes of the men who died flying it: CIA crew Walter Ray, Jack Weeks and Jim Zwayer and Lockheed test crew Ray Torick. The thirty surviving planes, many of which flew just a few hundred hours during their front-line careers, are all now in museums.

For all its sheer powers and personality, the Blackbird did essentially the same thing that the Lightning Bug did and which the Firefly would have done, given the chance: fly high over enemy territory in order to photograph military and industrial sites.

Yet when a Lightning Bug crashed on recovery in Taiwan or disappeared over the forests of South-East Asia, no one grieved. No wives got that dreaded visit from a somber Air Force officer with his cap tucked under his arm.

It should come as no surprise then, that the Air Force briefly combined the two concepts, pairing the fast but precious Blackbird with a speedy but disposable drone. The pairing of the Mach 3 spy plane with the Lockheed-made D-21 supersonic drone was unsuccessful, and even got one man killed.

Reconfigured to launch from a B-52, the D-21 flew operational missions over China between late 1969 and early 1971. None resulted in a single usable frame of film.

The D-21's abortive front-line service stands in contrast to the Model 147's long and productive career, and perhaps speaks for the wisdom of Ryan Aeronautical's evolutionary approach to drone development.

The Model 147 worked to the extent that it did because it was unspectacular. Notably, during the next wave of military drone development beginning in the 1990s, the most successful models were those that, like the Lightning Bug, slowly evolved from well-proven basic designs.

The D-21 was a direct response to the S-75, just like the Model 147. Chinese S-75s were plucking Taiwanese U-2s from the sky at an alarming rate when, in 1962, Lockheed designer Kelly Johnson traveled to Washington, D.C. to pitch the concept that would become the D-21.

Johnson had worked on both the U-2 and the SR-71. He wanted to develop a new reconnaissance aircraft with the sensor capabilities of a U-2 and the high speed of an SR-71 but without the major liability inherent in both designs: the on-board pilot.

The CIA rejected Johnson's drone proposal, but NRO head Brigadier General Leo Paul Geary liked it. Geary found $500,000 for development and Kelly got to work.

Harold Brown was the Air Force secretary at the time. A year prior, as the Defense Department's chief weapons-tester, Brown had canceled funding for the Model 147. However, he enthusiastically supported Johnson's high-speed drone concept.

With military support for the D-21 only growing, the CIA changed its mind in 1963 and joined the effort. The NRO, Air Force and CIA agreed to share responsibility for developing and tasking the new drone.

The program got a code-name: Tagboard. The NRO early on set aside $31 million for fifty vehicles. As development proceeded, costs rose and expectations diminished. The government ultimately poured more than $300 million into Tagboard and got out of it just thirty-three airframes.

Tagboard was highly classified. 'Even Skunk Works engineers working in the Fort Knox-like SR-71 assembly building were restricted from viewing the D-21 by a hangar bulkhead dubbed "Berlin Wall West",' historian Ehrhard noted.

Made of titanium and weighing 12 tons, the 19ft-wingspan D-21 in its early forms launched from atop a special variant of the A-12, the CIA's version of the SR-71. The A-12 in essence was the booster for the drone, climbing to 80,000ft of altitude and accelerating to Mach 3.3 before separating from the pilotless vehicle.

The D-21's ramjet engine took over, allowing it to cruise at three times the speed of sound for as far as 3,000 miles. A 300lb Hycon HR 335 camera peering through the drone's lower fuselage could capture 5,600 exposures covering an area 16 miles wide and 3,900 miles long.

The drone followed a pre-programmed flight path and maintained only intermittent radio contact with the launch plane that allowed an operator to monitor the drone's performance. As it reached its final waypoint, the D-21 jettisoned a capsule containing its exposed film and then self-destructed.

The film descended on a parachute. The plan was for a special JC-130 transport plane to snatch the parachute in mid-air. Failing that, a Navy ship could fish the capsule from the ocean.

The military and intelligence communities in the late 1960s hoped the D-21 would help the United States to spy on strategic targets more reliably than a satellite could do at that time, and without risking a human pilot.

'The Tagboard drone provides a unique technical capability to satisfy national requirements to conduct imagery reconnaissance operations against targets hostile or potentially hostile to the United States,' the Joint Chiefs of Staff explained in a September 1969 memo.

'In view of the political sensitivity to overflight of certain denied areas, such as China, by manned collection systems and the technical and other limitations of the current satellite program, the Tagboard operational capability has been developed to collect against objectives of national interest located in areas where manned operations could provoke incidents potentially embarrassing to the United States.'

Too bad that it didn't work. A fatal crash during July 1966 abruptly ended the effort to combine the A-12 and D-21. Desperate to salvage something from Tagboard, the NRO added a rocket booster to the D-21 and migrated the system to a small fleet of lightly-modified B-52H bombers.

By 1969 the D-21 was ready for action. China had tested its first atomic warhead in 1964. Washington was very interested in Beijing's nuclear facilities in southern China; facilities that satellites at the time failed adequately to survey. 'Ninety-three percent of the high-priority South China targets had no coverage during the previous two months,' the Joint Chiefs of Staff explained in their September 1969 memo.

The Joint Chiefs assumed China's radars would detect an incoming D-21, but Chinese S-75s 'are not considered to pose a threat to the Tagboard drone.'

The NRO oversaw four D-21 missions over China. The agency characterized all four as 'unsuccessful'. The third mission launched on March 4, 1971. Its results apparently are representative of the success of the overall program. The drone completed its recon run but failed to safely eject its film capsule.

'The parachute system was partially disabled by loss of the air pick-up chute which prevented an air snatch by the JC-130 aircraft,' the NRO reported to the Defense Department. 'There is a strong probability that a malfunctioning valve prevented adequate cooling of the parachute compartment during flight of the drone. The resultant overheat condition, sustained for over an hour, could have degraded the tensile strength of parachute components.'

'Although the main parachute canopy lowered the payload to the water surface, a subsequent pick-up attempt by a Navy vessel was unsuccessful due to procedural errors, and the payload sank.'

The NRO attempted one more D-21 mission over China on March 20, but it too ended in failure.

Meanwhile, politics intervened.

President Richard Nixon planned to visit China in 1972. In the same way that President Dwight Eisenhower's diplomatic overtures to the Soviets in the late 1950s curtailed manned US spy lights, Nixon's outreach to Communist China put the cap on the failing D-21 and Compass Arrow efforts. The Nixon administration in July 1971 ended all recce flights over China.

There was another factor in the softening support for the D-21 and Compass Arrow programs: satellites. This factor was also not new. Military leaders' early bullishness on space surveillance in the 1960s helped to curtail manned and unmanned aerial recon.

By mid-1971 the NRO had decided to entirely abandon aerial reconnaissance in favor of a purely satellite-based intelligence-collection effort. 'I have become increasingly convinced that we should be expending our efforts on upgrading our satellite activities, rather than trying to continue with air-breathing vehicles,' NRO director John McLucas wrote in an April 1971 memo.

McLucas noted that new spy satellites were spending more time in orbit. In 1971 Corona, Gambit and Hexagon spy sats would rack up a combined 181 days in orbit, McLucas reported. He projected days in orbit would grow to 279 by 1974.

Unsafe, unreliable drones were no longer necessary for strategic overhead reconnaissance, the NRO concluded. However, McLucas for one anticipated that drones might some day make a big comeback in a different mission. 'I believe that there is a weapons-carrying role for drones which ought to be exploited.'

Surviving D-21s reside at several US museums. China recovered the wreck of one self-destructed D-21 and put it on display in Beijing.

The 20ft-long drone at 2 tons fully loaded was small and lightweight. With its 530 miles per hour top speed, it was relatively slow. Its 60,000ft-plus ceiling was impressive in comparison to a fighter's ceiling, but was normal for a spy plane.

While hardly inexpensive at around $200,000 per copy in the mid-1960s, the drone was more or less disposable. The US military bought more than 1,000 Model 147s. Each on average completed fewer than four operational sorties before crashing or otherwise being written off.

Unloved by historians and aviation enthusiasts, the Model 147 faded into obscurity. The Lightning Bug's virtual erasure from the public record was complete when the Predator drone took to the sky over the Balkans in the mid-1990s and killed its first militant in Afghanistan in 2001. Many people assumed that military drones – in particular armed ones – were new.

They weren't new. Three decades earlier Ryan Aeronautical's Lightning Bugs played a major role in aerial espionage efforts over China and North Korea and, more prominently, in the air war over Vietnam.

The US Air Force in 1966 asked North American Aviation and Ryan Aeronautical to compete for the production of 100 new Compass Arrow recce drones that could fly as high as 80,000ft at a top speed of more than 600 miles per hour over a distance of 2,000 miles with a high degree of navigational accuracy and a payload of the latest long focal-length cameras. The Air Force separately commissioned General Electric to produce a new engine for the drone: the J97. (*Teledyne Ryan photo courtesy of the San Diego Air and Space Museum Archive*)

A US Air Force CH-3 helicopter recovers a Model 154 drone prototype. The 34ft-long drone featured a sharply-swept wing and all the high-tech features Ryan Aeronautical and the Air Force had developed for late-model Model 147s: contrail-suppression, jammers for defeating S-75 batteries, systems for automatic evasive maneuvers. While an impressive performer, the Model 154 was also outrageously expensive. (*Teledyne Ryan photo courtesy of the San Diego Air and Space Museum Archive*)

Development of the Model 154 was supposed to take just eighteen months starting in 1966 but instead stretched out over five years. The total cost swelled to $250 million while the production order shrank to just twenty-eight airframes, eight of which were test models. It didn't help that the drone had competition in the form of arguably the most famous manned spy plane that ever flew – the SR-71 Blackbird – as well as the super-fast D-21 drone that literally piggybacked on the Blackbird's success. (*Teledyne Ryan photo courtesy of the San Diego Air and Space Museum Archive*)

A foul-up in August 1969 blew the Model 154's cover. A Firefly's control-surface actuator malfunctioned as the drone soared over the White Sands Missile Range in New Mexico. The malfunction triggered automatic emergency procedures. The Firefly cut its engine and popped its orange-and-white recovery parachute. As the C-130 launch plane flew overhead, the drone floated down to a soft landing in a picnic area just inside the perimeter fence of the Los Alamos federal nuclear laboratory, close enough to adjacent residential neighborhoods for thousands of civilians to see it. Some took pictures. (*Teledyne Ryan photo courtesy of the San Diego Air and Space Museum Archive*)

The US Air Force in mid-1966 commissioned Ryan Aeronautical to develop the Model 154 drone specifically in order to spy on China's Lop Nor nuclear facility. The program embarrassed itself in August 1969 when a prototype Model 154's control-surface actuator malfunctioned as the drone soared over the White Sands Missile Range in New Mexico. The Model 154 cut its engine, popped its recovery parachute and landed in full view of the public just inside the fence of the Los Alamos federal nuclear laboratory. 'I don't like it, I don't like it,' muttered Major Ken Beckner, the pilot of the DC-130 mothership that launched the drone. (*Teledyne Ryan photo courtesy of the San Diego Air and Space Museum Archive*)

News crews were already gathering when a combined US Air Force and Ryan Aeronautical crew arrived to begin recovering the Model 154 prototype that accidentally landed at the Los Alamos federal nuclear laboratory in New Mexico in August 1969. It would take the crew twenty-eight hours of work to disassemble the drone, crane it onto a rented truck, haul it to Santa Fe and load it onto the C-130. Associated Press reporter Bill Stockton rushed out a dispatch. 'Reverberations from the thud of the graceful bird's landing on the northern New Mexico mountain plateau … was felt all the way to Washington,' Stockton wrote. (*Teledyne Ryan photo courtesy of the San Diego Air and Space Museum Archive*)

Shortly after a Model 154 prototype accidentally landed at the Los Alamos federal nuclear laboratory in New Mexico in August 1969, photos of the drone ended up at the office of the *Los Alamos Monitor* newspaper. Government agents pressed editor Markly McMahon to turn over the photos, but he declined. 'It's not every day that you see a plane coming down on a big orange-and-white double parachute with a C-130 Air Force plane circling over the town,' McMahon said. A year later trade magazine *Aviation Week* published a story accurately detailing the Model 154's appearance and capabilities. (*Teledyne Ryan photo courtesy of the San Diego Air and Space Museum Archive*)

San Diego artist Robert Watts was Ryan Aeronautical's lead illustrator from the mid-1960s through the mid-1970s. He produced beautiful illustrations of the company's drone types for internal use as well as for ads and other marketing. This 1973 painting depicts a Model 154 on its trolley as well as, in the background, a DC-130 mothership. (*Teledyne Ryan photo courtesy of the San Diego Air and Space Museum Archive*)

Conceived by Lockheed Martin's Skunk Works division, the D-21 was an unmanned Mach 3 reconnaissance vehicle that the company initially designed to launch from the back of an M-21 manned carrier aircraft, itself a variant of the A-12, the predecessor of the SR-71 spy plane. (*Lockheed Martin photo*)

The D-21 was originally designed to launch at supersonic speed from the back of an M-21 carrier aircraft. In July 1966, a D-21 collided with its M-21 after release, destroying both and resulting in the death of one of the M-21's two crew members. No further 'piggyback' launches were attempted. (*US Air Force photo*)

The operational launch system used modified B-52H carrier aircraft. The D-21B had a solid rocket booster to provide the initial acceleration required to start the ramjet engine. The first launch from a B-52 took place in 1967. (*US Air Force photo*)

# Bibliography/Sources

**Primary Sources:**

Bell, T.E., *B-57 Canberra Units of the Vietnam War* (Bloomsbury Publishing, 2013)
Bergin, Bob, 'The Growth of China's Air Defenses: Responding to Covert Overflights, 1949–1974' (*Studies in Intelligence*, June 2013)
Boyne, Walter J., 'Linebacker II' (*Air Force Magazine*, July 19, 2008)
Butz, J.S., Jr., 'The Need to Know', (*Air Force & Space Digest*, January 1963)
Cahill, William, 'Strategic Air Command SIGINT Support to the Vietnam War' (*Air Power History*, Winter 2019)
Crickmore, Paul, *Lockheed Blackbird: Beyond the Secret Missions* (Osprey Publishing, 2016)
Davies, Peter, *F-105 Wild Weasel vs SA-2 'Guideline' SAM: Vietnam 1965–73*
Doubek, Major Thomas, *Strategic Reconnaissance 1956–1976: A History of the 4080th/100th SRW* (Taylor Publishing Company, 1976)
Ellsberg, Daniel, *Secrets: A Memoir of Vietnam and the Pentagon Papers* (Penguin, 2003)
*Foreign Relations of the United States, 1964–1968*, Volume III, *Vietnam, June–December 1965* (US State Department Office of the Historian: https://history.state.gov/historicaldocuments/frus1964-68v03/d71)
Hanyok, Robert, 'Skunks, Bogies, Silent Hounds and the Flying Fish: The Gulf of Tonkin Mystery, 2-4 August 1964' (*Cryptologic Quarterly*, 2001)
McCarthy, James, Allison, George and Rayfield, Robert, *Linebacker II: A View from the Rock*
Michel, Marshall III, *Operation Linebacker II 1972* (Bloomsbury Publishing, 2018)
Nalty, Bernard, 'The Air Force in South-East Asia: Tactics and Techniques of Electronic Warfare' (Office of Air Force History)
Sloggett, Dave, *Drone Warfare: The Development of Unmanned Aerial Conflict* (Pen and Sword, 2014)
Trevithick, Joseph, 'The US Army's First Drone Bases Were Simple', *War Is Boring*, (February 27, 2017: https://medium.com/war-is-boring/the-u-s-armys-first-drone-bases-were-easy-and-simple-4b8438c55523)
'U-2 Overflights and the Capture of Francis Gary Powers, 1960' (US State Department Office of the Historian, https://history.state.gov/milestones/1953-1960/u2-incident)
Wagner, William, 'Lightning Bugs and Other Reconnaissance Drones' (*Armed Forces Journal International* in cooperation with Aero Publishers Inc., 1982)
Wagner, William and Sloan, William, *Fireflies and Other UAVs* (Aerofax Inc., 1992)
Zaloga, Steven, 'Defending the Kremlin' (*Journal of Slavic Military Studies*, 1997)
Zaloga, Steven, *Red SAM: The SA-2 Guideline Anti-Aircraft Missile* (Osprey Publishing, 2007)

**Secondary Sources:**

Chief, Plans for Field Activities, OSA, CIA, Memorandum for the Record, Subject: LONG ARM Drone Modifications, August 13, 1965

Johnson, Lyndon B., 'By Lyndon B. Johnson: Bombing North After Tonkin Attack' (*New York Times*, October 20, 1971

'May Day Over Moscow: The Francis Gary Powers Story', Central Intelligence Agency, 2015: https://www.cia.gov/news-information/featured-story-archive/2015-featured-story-archive/francis-gary-powers.html

*On Watch: Profiles of the National Security Agency's Past 40 Years*

'Pilotless US Plane Downed, China Says' (*New York Times*, November 17, 1964)

'The Radar Warning Story', Northrop Grumman Corporation promotional material: https://www.aef.se/Avionik/Artiklar/Motmedel/Nya_hotbilder/RadarWarnStory.pdf

Rowe, Peter, 'Bobbi Swan, a pioneer in drone technology and sexual identity, 1930–2018' (*San Diego Union Tribune*, January 8, 2019)

Technical Report APA-TR-2009-0702, 'Almaz S-75 Dvina/Desna/Volkhov Air-Defense System/HQ-2A/B/CSA-1/SA-2 Guideline' by Dr Carlo Kopp, July 2009: https://www.ausairpower.net/APA-S-75-Volkhov.html#mozTocId912634

US and Soviet statements and diplomatic cables, reprinted as part of Yale Law School's Avalon Project: Documents in Law, History and Diplomacy: https://avalon.law.yale.edu/20th_century/u2.asp

'VIETCONG GAINS LAUDED IN CHINA; Article Calls 1964 a Year of American Defeats' (*New York Times*, December 27, 1964)

# Index

100th Strategic Reconnaissance Wing, 98, 123, 137
112th Fighter Group, 19
318th Fighter-Interceptor Squadron, 19
4080th Strategic Reconnaissance Wing, 50–5, 57, 60, 70–2, 76, 83, 87, 123

A-1 attack plane, 72
A-2 camera, 6–7
A-4 attack plane, 127
A-12 spy plane, 147–8, 158
Afghanistan, vii, 129, 138, 150
AGM-65 missile, 129, 133–4
*Air Force & Space Digest*, 12
AN/APR-26 radar-warning receiver, 81, 85, 95
AN/ALQ-51 jammer, 95
AN/ALT-22 jammer, 135
AN/ALT-28 jammer, 136
AN/ALT-6B jammer, 135
Anderson, Rudolph, 30
Applied Technology, 81, 85, 95
AR-15 rifle, 70, 72
Associated Press, 145, 155
Atterberry, Edwin, 8
*Aviation Week*, 146, 156

B-24 bomber, 44
B-26 bomber, 21–2, 26
B-29 bomber, 1
B-52 bomber, 87, 123, 128–30, 134–7, 143, 146, 148, 159
B-57 bomber, 3, 9–10, 34, 72, 77
B-camera, 12
*Baby Buck*, 26
The Balkans, 138, 149
Ball, George, 38
Ballweg, Ray, 4, 9
Barometric low-altitude control system, 82, 112
Beck, A.J., 54, 55
Beckner, Ken, 145, 154
Beijing, 34, 69, 72–3, 75, 148, 149

Bell, T.E., 72
*Bennington*, USS, 122, 125–6
Bergin, Bob, 29
Berlin, 28, 147
Bernasconi, Louis, 136
Bien Hoa air base, 50, 56–7, 69–73, 76–7, 79, 82, 86, 88, 98, 103
*Big Red*, 26
Big Safari, 30, 108, 144
Bissell, Jr, Richard, 3, 5
Blanchard, Wiliam, 31
Brinks Hotel, 78
Brown, Harold, 27, 147
*Budweiser*, 26
Burzynski, Norman, 19
Butz, J.S., 12

C-47 transport, 72
C-119 transport, 89–90
D/G/C-130 transport/mothership, vii, 11, 14, 20–1, 23, 30–1, 50–4, 56, 58–9, 62–4, 70–2, 76, 83, 87–9, 98, 106, 129, 135, 137, 140, 142, 145, 148, 153–7
C-133 transport, 51
Cahill, William, 81
Castro, Fidel, 29
Central Intelligence Agency, vii, 2–3, 5, 13, 28–33, 80, 83, 146–7
Charyk, Joseph, 30–1
China, viii, 3, 23, 29, 34, 38–9, 52–5, 60, 65, 69, 70, 72–5, 110, 146, 148–50, 154
Chinese Communist Party, 72–3, 75
Christian, Ed, 96–7, 109, 117
Combat Dawn, 107, 119
Compass Cookie, 135
Congress, 1, 38, 40, 50
Conlee, Bill, 136
Conover, David, 43, 46
Corona satellite, 3, 10, 89, 149
Corra, Andy, 107
Cuba, 29–33, 79

D-21 drone, vii, 34, 146–49, 152, 158–9
Da Nang, 68, 70–1, 87, 97
Davis-Monthan Air Force Base, 50, 86
The Dayton-Wright Airplane Company, 43
Decai, Han, 29
Defense Intelligence Agency, 106
Denny, Reginald, 43
Desoto, Operation, 39
DesPortes, John, 54–6, 63, 65
Doppler radar, 53, 64, 88
Doubek, Thomas, 52, 71
Dougherty, Norma Jeane, 43–4, 46
D/P-2 mothership, 21, 24

E-2 radar plane, 122–3
Eastman Kodak Company, 7
EB-66 reconnaissance plane, 41, 80
EC-121 reconnaissance plane, 106–107, 119
Eisenhower, Dwight, 3, 5, 27–8, 30, 149
*Elath*, 121
Electronic intelligence, 41, 107, 119
Emrich, Daniel, 51
Explosive ordnance disposal, 97

R/F-4 fighter/reconnaissance plane, 7–8, 79, 85, 129, 138, 140
F-8 fighter, 39, 42
F-86 fighter, 17
F-100 fighter, 17, 98
F-102 fighter, 19
F-105 fighter, 79
F-106 fighter, 30
Fairchild, 89
Fan Song radar, 79–80, 95–6, 102, 130
Field Goal, Operation, 129
Fire Bee II drone, 141
Fubini, Eugene, 41, 80

Gambit satellite, 149
Gates, Thomas, 27
General Electric, 144, 150
Glienicke Bridge, 28
Great War, The, 43
Grechko, S.N., 29–30
Guam, 51–2, 55, 128, 134–5
Gulf of Tonkin, 1, 38–40, 42, 51, 106, 121–2, 127–8, 136
Gulf of Tonkin Resolution, 50

H-1 helicopter, 70–1
H-3 helicopter, 90–3, 97, 151

H-37 helicopter, 68, 91
H-43 helicopter, 72
Hainan Island, 51, 123
Haiphong Harbor, 57, 82, 88, 106
Hanoi, 7, 8, 39, 40, 79, 82, 115, 127, 129–31, 135–7
Hanyok, Robert, 40
Harpoon missile, 121, 124
Hat Rack, 96, 100
Helmich, Bill, 129, 131
Herter, Christian, 28
Hexagon satellite, 149
Hill Air Force Base, 137
Hoa Lo Prison, 127
Hobbs, Lisa, 73
Holloman Air Force Base, 13, 22–3, 30
HR233 camera, 6, 88–9
HR335 camera, 147
HR732 camera, 6–7
Hycon 73B camera, 12
Hycon Manufacturing, 4, 6, 9, 11, 12, 20, 65, 69, 88–9, 147

*I Go Pogo No. IV*, 26
India, 29
Iraq, 58, 138
Israel, 121, 139

J69 engine, 11, 15, 17, 35, 44, 81, 95–6, 100
J97 engine, 144, 150
Jackson, Robert, 63–5, 69
Japan, 51, 73, 107
Johnson, Kelly, 34, 147
Johnson, Lyndon, 1, 38–40, 50, 72, 76, 86, 128, 129
Joint Chiefs of Staff, 38, 41, 72, 86, 106, 148

KA-60 camera, 6, 89
Kadena Air Force Base, 51, 53–4, 56, 59, 62
Kennedy, John F., 1, 27, 28, 30, 39
Kennedy, Joseph Jr., 44
Kettering Aerial Torpedo, 43
Kettering, Charles, 43
Khrushchev, Nikita, 3, 27–30
KS-54 camera, 44
KS-61 camera, 44

Laos, 38, 55, 83
Leaflets, vii, 129–30
LeMay, Curtis, 13, 27, 31
Linebacker II, 130, 134–7

Litton Industries, 11–12, 46
Lockheed Martin Corporation, 158
Lockheed Martin Skunk Works, 158
Long Arm, Operation, 32–3, 38, 41, 79–81, 85
Long-range radio navigation aids, 64
Lop Nor nuclear site, viii, 144, 154
Los Alamos federal nuclear laboratory, 145, 153–6
*Los Alamos Monitor*, 145, 156
Los Angeles, 43, 46
Lucast, Jack, 51–2, 54–5

M-21 mothership, 158–9
*Maddox*, USS, 1, 38–9, 42
Martin, Edward, 127–8
Massachusetts Institute of Technology, 10, 37
Mayall, William, 136
McChord Air Force Base, 19
McLucas, John, 149
McMahon, Markly, 145, 156
Mid-air retrieval system, 89–90, 93, 94, 122–3, 137, 140
MiG-17 fighter, 29, 82
MiG-21 fighter, 84, 106
Military Museum of the Chinese People's Revolution, 34, 63, 75
Missile Development Center, 23
Model 136 drone, 13
Model 147A drone, 30–1, 36, 96, 104, 108
Model 147B drone, 23, 31–3, 36, 41, 51, 54–5, 60, 62–3, 67–8, 70–1, 73, 79, 81–2, 86, 95
Model 147C drone, 32, 79, 82–3, 87
Model 147D drone, 32–3, 38, 41, 79–80
Model 147E drone, 33, 38, 41, 79–80, 95, 130
Model 147F drone, 95
Model 147G drone, 81–3, 86–7, 95, 100, 103
Model 147H drone, 81, 95–7, 99–103, 103, 107, 110, 118–19, 135
Model 147J drone, 6, 87, 88–9, 95, 96, 99, 103, 107, 112
Model 147N drone, 86–7, 96
Model 147NA drone, 109
Model 147NC drone, 109, 120, 129–30
Model 147NP drone, 96
Model 147NRE drone, 96–7, 104, 108
Model 147NX drone, 103
Model 147SA drone, 108
Model 147SB drone, 108
Model 147SC drone, 26, 107, 114–15, 122, 136
Model 147SC/TV drone, 129

Model 147SK drone, 122–3, 125–6
Model 147SRE drone, 104, 108
Model 147SRE-2 drone, 109, 117
Model 147T drone, 67, 107, 118–19
Model 147TE drone, 107, 118–19, 141
Model 154 drone, 144, 146, 151–7
Model 234A drone, 124, 128–9, 132–4
Model 248 drone, 121
Model 255 drone, 120
Moscow, 1–3, 32
MQ-1 Predator drone, vii–viii
Mulligan, James, 137
Multiple altitude control system, 108, 112–13

National Aeronautics and Space Administration, 27
National Reconnaissance Office, 30, 89, 144–5, 147–9
National Security Agency, vii, 39–40, 106–107, 119
*The New York Times*, 40, 73
Nixon, Richard, 27, 107, 128, 137, 149
North American Aviation, 144, 150
North Atlantic Treaty Organization, 2, 137, 140
North Korea, 1–2, 106, 107, 118–19, 150
North Vietnam, 7, 26, 38–9, 41, 51, 70, 74, 79–82, 84, 95, 108–109, 115, 123, 128–30, 134, 137–9
Nuclear weapons, 1, 10, 28–31, 69

Okinawa, 51–6, 63
Old Bar, Operation, 81
Omaha, 51, 54, 65
Omar, Mullah, vii, viii
Operating Location 8, 51–6, 63
Operating Location 16, 107, 119
Operating Location 20, 56, 71–2, 74, 81–2, 95, 97, 103, 106, 121, 129
Oplan 34A, 39
OQ-2 drone, 18, 43–4, 47
OQ-3 drone, 43, 47
Orr, Bill, 9
Osan air base, 107, 119, 137, 141

Pakistan, 3, 29
Parrott, Thomas, 8
Perkins, Courtland, 11, 25, 31
The Philippines, 51, 79, 122
Powers, Gary, 3–4, 27–9
Powers, Thomas, 31

*Pueblo*, USS, 107
Puerto Rico, 24
Purple Dragon, Operation, 106

Q-2 drone, 9, 11–12, 19, 21–2, 35, 45, 89–90
Q-2C drone, 9, 11, 13–18, 20, 23–4, 26, 30–1, 35–6, 44–5, 51, 121–2, 143
Q-2D drone, 13

R-14 missile, 29–30
RB-47 reconnaissance plane, 32, 38, 41, 79–80
Radar-absorbing material, 13, 96, 100–101
Radioplane Company, The, 43, 46–7
*Ranger*, USS, 122–3
Reichardt, Bob, 71–2, 74, 87, 108
RF-101 reconnaissance plane, 79, 82, 84
Rivet Bounder, 96, 100, 102
Ryan Aeronautical Company, vii, 4, 6, 9–13, 15–16, 20–1, 25–7, 30–3, 35–6, 41, 44–5, 50–6, 59–61, 63–5, 70–1, 81–3, 86–90, 95–6, 100–101, 104–109, 111, 116–19, 121–3, 128–9, 131–2, 141, 143–6, 150–1, 154–5, 157
*Ryan's Daughter*, 26
Ryan, Lloyd, 4, 9, 31, 50, 52–3
Ryan, T.C., 9

S-25 Berkut surface-to-air missile system, 1–3
S-75 surface-to-air missile system, 2–4, 7, 29, 30, 32–4, 41, 63, 70, 74, 79–85, 95, 102, 109, 127, 130, 136–8, 147, 148, 151
Saigon, viii, 56–7, 69, 71, 76, 78, 87, 137, 141
San Diego, 4, 11–12, 14–25, 27, 35–7, 41, 51, 55, 58–60, 62, 64, 67–8, 71–2, 75, 91–4, 98–104, 108, 110–11, 115–16, 118–20, 122, 124–6, 128, 131–4, 139–41, 150–7
Schwanhausser, Robert, 10–13, 16, 27, 35, 37, 44, 45, 51–2, 54–6, 63–6, 69–71, 74, 80, 82, 87, 95, 138, 144
SD-1 drone, 44, 48–9
Second World War, vii, 1, 9–10, 43–4, 47, 72, 122, 125
Smith, Harold, 86
SNR-75 radar, 2
South China Sea, 38, 51, 63
South Korea, 107, 119, 137, 141
South Vietnam, 1, 38–9, 50, 56, 70, 72, 74, 76, 78–9, 89, 97, 98, 103, 106–107, 128, 134, 137
Soviet Union, 1–3, 7, 28–9, 31, 79
Space Technology Labs, 11
SR-71 spy plane, vii, 10, 56, 146–7, 152, 158

Stalin, Joseph, 1–2
Stockton, Bill, 145, 155
Strategic Air Command, 31, 33, 37–8, 41, 50–2, 54–7, 63, 65, 69–71, 74, 79–82, 86–7, 92, 96–7, 109–10, 128, 130, 134–6
Strategic Arms Limitation Treaty II, 138
Styx missile, 121
Sved, Bill, 64
Swan, Bobbi, 37, 138

Tactical Air Command, 30, 109, 129, 137, 140
Taiwan, 3, 29, 34, 51–5, 63, 65–70, 146–7
Tet Offensive, 97
Thailand, 37, 98, 123, 128, 134, 136–8, 141
*Ticonderoga*, USS, 39, 42
*Tom Cat*, 26, 107, 114–16
Traveling wave tube, 80, 86
Tsygankov, M., 79
Tyndall Air Force Base, 31, 141

U Tapao air base, 98, 123, 128, 130, 134–5, 137, 141
U-2 spy plane, 2
Uhl, Edward, 9–10
U.S. Air Force, vii, 1–2, 4–13, 15, 17, 19, 21–3, 25–6, 30–1, 33, 37–8, 41, 49–54, 56–59, 61–2, 64–5, 68, 71–9, 81–2 84–7, 89–91, 95–6, 98, 100, 105, 107–109, 112–14, 117, 120, 123–4, 128–2, 134–5, 137–8, 141–2, 144–7, 150–1, 154–6, 159
U.S. Army, 1, 10, 38, 43–4, 46–9, 54, 68, 70–1, 89–91, 106
U.S. Marine Corps, 68, 96–7
U.S. Navy, 1, 21, 23–4, 30, 38–9, 42–4, 47, 51, 58, 68, 71, 79, 81, 91, 95, 106–107, 109, 121–5, 127–8, 137, 142–3, 148–9
Utility Squadron 5, 51
Utility Squadron 8, 24

V-300 missile, 2
V-750 missile, 2–4, 30, 32, 41, 57, 80–2, 85, 95–6, 108–109, 112–13, 117, 127, 130, 135
Van Minh, Duong, 137, 141
Van Nuys Airport, 43, 46
Viet Cong, 1, 68, 71, 73, 76–8, 96–8

Wagner, William, 31, 59, 64, 74, 82–3, 86–7, 97, 144
Warner Robins Air Force Base, 137
Watts, Robert, 116, 157

Weaver, Dale, 70–1, 80–2, 86, 97, 109, 123, 135, 145
Wheeler, Earle, 106
White Sands Missile Range, 13, 17, 145, 153–4
Wide World Photos, 73–4
William Tell exercise, 141

Yankee Station, 122
Yochim, Fred, 50, 89
Yom Kippur War, 139
Yuill, John, 136

Zaloga, Steven, 2–3
Zimmer, Terry, 72